7.00

...nts

...Go Your Way!

In *WINNING* you'll examine how to handle parents and employees, spouses and children, bosses and clients, lawyers and muggers and pests. You'll learn how to win by listening, how to argue and when not to. You'll see what *seems* to be happening in each case and then look behind the scenes at what else may be going on quietly, unrecognized. You'll develop a new way of dealing with the world around you so that you can finally get what you want. Where you feel you're the underdog, this book will help you get an even chance; where you're even, it'll give you the edge.

The first decision you must make is that you really want to win. You do, don't you?

Come on. Winning means becoming the very best you can be. The winner's circle is waiting for you—now!

WINNING

DAVID VISCOTT, M.D., is the bestselling author of: *The Making of a Psychiatrist, The Language of Feelings, How to Live with Another Person, Risking, Taking Care of Business* and *The Viscott Method* (ALL AVAILABLE FROM POCKET BOOKS). He hosts one of America's most popular syndicated radio talk shows, enjoyed by millions of listeners across the country. Dr. Viscott lives in Los Angeles, California.

Books by David S. Viscott, M.D.

Feel Free
How to Live with Another Person
The Language of Feelings
The Making of a Psychiatrist
Risking
Taking Care of Business
The Viscott Method: A Revolutionary Program
  for Self-Analysis and Self-Understanding
Winning

Published by POCKET BOOKS

Most Pocket Books are available at special quantity
discounts for bulk purchases for sales promotions, pre-
miums or fund raising. Special books or book excerpts
can also be created to fit specific needs.

For details write the office of the Vice President of
Special Markets, Pocket Books, 1230 Avenue of the
Americas, New York, New York 10020.

WINNING

Formerly titled:
HOW TO MAKE WINNING YOUR LIFESTYLE

David Viscott, M.D.

PUBLISHED BY POCKET BOOKS NEW YORK

For Elizabeth, Penelope, and Jonathan,
who are already Winners

Originally published in hardcover by Peter H. Wyden and in paperback by Dell Publishing Company, Inc.

Original title: *How To Make WINNING Your Lifestyle*

POCKET BOOKS, a division of Simon & Schuster, Inc.
1230 Avenue of the Americas, New York, N.Y. 10020

Published by arrangement with the author
Library of Congress Catalog Card Number: 73-189526

ISBN: 0-671-62050-9

First Pocket Books printing March 1987

10 9 8 7 6 5 4 3 2

POCKET and colophon are trademarks of Simon & Schuster, Inc.

Cover art based on a design © American Greetings Corporation

Printed in the U.S.A.

CONTENTS

CONTENTS

Nothing great was ever achieved
without enthusiasm.

—Emerson

A Bill of Rights For Winners

1. You have the right to be you—the way you are, the way you want to be.
2. You have the right to grow, to change, to become, to strive, to reach for any goal, to be limited only by your degree of talent and amount of effort.
3. You have the right to privacy—in a marriage, in a family, in any relationship, in any group—the right to keep a part of your life secret, no matter how trivial or how important, merely because you want it to be that way. And you have the right to be alone part of each day, each week, and each year, to spend time with yourself.
4. You have the right to be loved and to love, to be accepted, cared for, and adored, and you have the right to fulfill that right.
5. You have the right to ask questions, of anyone, at any time, in any matter that affects your life, so long as it is your business to do so, and to be listened to and taken seriously.
6. You have the right to self-respect and to do everything you need to do to increase your self-esteem so long as you hurt no one in doing so.
7. You have the right to be happy, to find something in the world that is meaningful and rewarding to you and gives you a sense of completeness.
8. You have the right to be trusted and to trust and to be taken at your word. If you were wrong, you have the right to be given a chance to make good, if possible.
9. You have the right to be free as long as you act responsibly and are mindful of the rights of others and of those obligations that you entered into freely.
10. You have the right to win, to succeed, to make plans, to see those plans fulfilled, to become the best you that you can possibly become.

1 / YOU CAN MAKE LIFE
GO YOUR WAY

IT'S PAINFUL TO ADMIT, but unless something drastic happens to you, you probably won't find yourself in the winner's circle this year either. You'll keep on making the same old mistakes and miss your best opportunities while others capitalize on theirs. You'll still be afraid to assert your rights, you'll let people take advantage of you and end up not getting what you want. And if you run true to form, you'll find plenty of excuses for not winning, excuses that may get you off the hook, but still won't get you what you want. You'll still believe it was just bum luck that things went wrong; or that the time wasn't right; or that someone got in your way again and kept you from winning.

Well, it's about time you face the facts. If anyone is keeping you from being a winner it's probably you, and unless you do something about it it'll be the same next year and the year after.

Look around at the people you admire, the people who get the big breaks, the ones who appear to be in control of their own destiny, who seem to have everything go their way. How do they do it? How do they find their way to the top and how do they stay there? After all, they don't seem that different from you.

There's No Such Thing As a Born Loser

It *is* possible to start winning and have things go your way for a change, in spite of how unlikely this may seem to you. Perhaps you think you are a born loser. That's what a lot of losers like to think, because people learn to expect less of losers and so the losers don't have to try so hard. Perhaps you believe that you have to be *born* with winning ways.

If so, you are wrong, because it *is* possible to learn the knack of winning. It is possible to change from being a loser to becoming a winner.

Perhaps you think that winning is mostly a matter of charisma or luck. Wrong again. Charisma is a knack, and everyone has luck. The key is that winners know it when they see it and know how to take advantage of it. And you can learn that, too, right here and now.

Is it really all that difficult to make the right decision at the right time? It just couldn't be. Look at people who are more successful than you. Do you sometimes say to yourself, "What's wrong with me? I'm as smart as he is! I could have figured out what he did. I could have done the very same thing!" The irony is that you are probably right. And even if you're not as smart as the other fellow, you're smart enough to make a success of yourself.

How much brains do you think it takes to be successful? It's not brains that determine success. There are professors on skid row and a lot of geniuses who can't get ahead. So it can't be brains alone that guarantee success.

Even though most people are capable of doing better, they are inept and manage to bungle (more or less) nearly everything important in their lives. Nobody likes to think of himself as incompetent, but in managing their personal affairs, that is largely the way people are.

What Kind of Decision-Maker Are You?

Consider for a moment the most significant decisions you've made in your life, the ones that determined how you were to live, what you would do, and with whom: choosing a job, a spouse, or a home. Although you probably thought you knew what you were doing at the time and have convinced yourself by now that you did, you probably didn't. Just as you believe you know what you're doing most of the time now. Be honest about it. Like most people, you landed where you are more by chance than by planning. And that's why you need help now to learn to win—and not to expect it to happen by chance.

Did you ever feel after an unpleasant experience that if you could somehow have acted differently you might have been spared much misery? It's a common feeling. Unfortunately, by the time you reexamine your actions and are able to recognize your errors and the opportunities you missed, it is usually too late to do anything about them.

When you look back on the past you can see events more clearly and in more accurate perspective because you are not so inhibited by your emotions of the present. Decisions in the present invariably involve some risk; you could lose as a result of making the wrong choice. This fear of losing makes you feel uneasy, so you doubt your ability, and you don't function as effectively as you might. You may therefore be unable to discover and control the important factors that determine success.

Ineptness prevails mainly when people feel anxious, even if they are alert. A man may sell his house too cheaply if he is *afraid* he will not get a better offer. Under pressure, what you perceive and believe is colored by what you feel at the moment. *Fear* changes your ability to know the truth. The stress created by making large decisions often makes people act irrationally because the *fear* of losing obscures the real issue.

3

There Is a Winning Formula

There is a way to discover which details are important, to increase your insight into the present, to sharpen your effectiveness at making winning decisions. There is a way to be in control and not at the mercy of the moment. This is the winning way that this book is all about.

When people make major decisions they should be aware of the long-range effects—but they seldom are. Everyone is familiar with bungling of gigantic proportions in international politics; millions of people are placed in jeopardy and the peace of the world is threatened as the result of some leader's lack of perspective. Most of these crises appear idiotic. How do these leaders allow such situations to get out of hand?

The answer is absurdly simple. Great countries are run by men and women like you and me. They are motivated by the very same feelings, and, therefore, are just as likely to panic under pressure and make the wrong move. However, when ordinary people feel threatened by a situation beyond their capacity, they merely drink too much or ruin a round of golf, or tell an off-color story to the minister's wife. Ordinary people do not order armies into the field or drive families off their land. Our feelings of inadequacy are the same as those of national leaders. Only the means for converting our feelings into action are different. In either case the mishandled feelings cause disaster. In either case there is room for improvement.

When people act out of a sense of panic, falsely believing that they absolutely *must* act, *must* get married or divorced or blow their top, they may actually just be trying to avoid being passive or weak. Thus motivated, they often stick rigidly with their decisions, good or bad, and compound their mistakes. Yet when a decision is less important and people are less anxious, the important details are also likely to be overlooked. In that case, the wrong decision is made not from distorting the facts, or out of panic, but through carelessness and sloppiness.

The major decisions in life that are frequently mishandled—such as deciding whether to quit a job or to live less expensively—often wouldn't need to be made at all if prior decisions had been made properly in the first place.

The Billiard Champion's Technique

The first time I saw a professional pocket-billiard championship I was struck by how easy each shot seemed to be. Not that the players made the shots look easy. Most of the shots *were* in fact easy. Anyone with a few hours' experience could have put perhaps half of the balls away. What was difficult was controlling the cue ball and *lining up the next shot*. To make each following shot easy was enormously difficult. The good player knows that his future shots depend on his present one. He never acts for the moment, never takes a shot just because it is easy. He knows he must set up the next one. If he did not, each shot would become increasingly difficult.

If you are unaware of the influence that one event has on another in life and act without regard for the future, making one ill-advised decision after another, the time is guaranteed to come when you will be faced with a decision that is beyond your ability to solve. Although this may be the first time you are *aware* of making a bungled decision, it will not be the first time you have done so. It is the result of all your previous ineptness coming home to roost, the backlash of all the small details you ignored; you did not realize they were important because they carried you in the wrong direction.

And Are Your Goals Defined?

You can't win unless you know what you want. Most people don't fulfill their goals because they have never clearly defined them. If you haven't decided what your goals in life are, it is much more difficult to know what you want and make up your mind in any situation. Look at all the times when you acted out of ignorance and fear and chose a path because it seemed easier and less threatening—like not asking for a raise. Or perhaps you chose an unnecessarily difficult route just because you felt it was expected of you or felt that you had to prove yourself—like buying a house you couldn't afford. Neither of these choices would help you reach your goals. Would you make those choices now, knowing what you now know?

The chances are that you might, and for two reasons. First, although you know much more about yourself now than you used to, you probably haven't taken stock of your goals lately. You know mainly how events turned out in the past. Second, you are almost as likely to become anxious and to misinterpret the events happening about you now as you were then. If this vicious circle is to be broken, you'll need a new plan!

Needed: A Guide to Your Blind Spots

You need to bring a new kind of objectivity into your present life to see your present world more clearly. You need to be able to act, knowing what is going on inside you and inside the people around you. You need some guide lines to help you manage your blind spots.

The new perspective you need is to be able to look at the present from the viewpoint of the future, your future.

You can make events go your way, start winning, and stop goofing up. In the chapters that follow you are going to take a new look at the way people bungle everyday situations in their personal and professional lives. I'll show you the mistakes people make and why. You'll learn how to manage others so they don't get in your way. You'll discover how to go about solving crucial problems that you may now handle as blithely as you choose one brand of toothpaste over another because you're unaware of their importance. You'll become aware of the ways people undermine each other, and you'll discover how you sabotage yourself. More important, you'll discover new, alternative ways to act, and how and why they work.

This book is a guide to help you get the upper hand and keep it. And the first person over whom you must get the upper hand is yourself. Here you'll learn how. Perhaps you'll see some of your own past mistakes more clearly and learn to maintain your distance and your sense of humor. Perhaps you'll get a look into the future.

I'll examine how to handle parents and employees, spouses and children, bosses and clients, lawyers and muggers and pests. You'll learn how to win by listening, how to argue, and when not to. You'll see what *seems* to be happening in each case and then look behind the scenes at what else may be going on quietly, unrecognized. The object of this book is to help you develop a new way of dealing with the world around you so that you can finally get what you want. Where you feel you're the underdog this book will help you get an even chance; where you're even, it'll give you the edge.

The first decision you must make is that you really want to win. You do, don't you?

Look, all you have to lose is your losing ways. Come on. Winning means becoming the very best you you can be. The winner's circle has been waiting for much too long.

WINNERS KNOW SOMETHING you probably don't. Besides knowing how to win, they know how to keep their losses to a minimum. And that's not really the same thing.

Many people believe they must act quickly to make a decision or take a chance. Sometimes this is true; more often, all it takes to win is to avoid making mistakes that would soon have become obvious to you if you had waited. Winners wait until they have a better understanding of what they want; what they have; what the situation really offers. They hold on just a little bit before they commit themselves.

Tool No. 1: Understand the Present Situation

You're probably in better shape now than you think. That's right. You probably have more strengths, more aces up your sleeve than you're aware of. Look: you've survived this far. That speaks for some ability, doesn't it?

In a world as complicated as this, you have been exposed to bills, bosses, babies, relatives, traffic, disease, pain, sorrow, and joy. Even if you think you're unsuccessful in life, you've learned something from your experience, even if you believe it was all bad, even if you believe that you ruined everything you touched. In a primitive society you might even be king for knowing what you know now. And you can do a great deal more in this society if you learn the right way to use what you know.

Your experience has given you some understanding of what you are like and what you want. You *do* know more now than you used to. The problem is to find a way to make that knowledge work more constructively so that you don't fall back into your old ruts again.

The winner knows who he is and knows what he has. He also knows that to jump blindly at an opportunity is to risk throwing away everything he has worked for.

Winners know that they are human and that to be human means to be capable of making mistakes. But instead of waiting for others to point out those mistakes they look for them themselves. Because they are aware that they can misjudge events, they are cautious and always question themselves: how could a decision harm them? Only then do they consider the good side. Pessimistic? Hardly. It's just one of a winner's realistic ways.

Tool No. 2: Take Your Time

Very few issues are so urgent that they must be decided at once. Very few quick decisions work out right, although people tend to remember the spectacular ones that do, and envy those who make them. There are many more spectacular failures that you are far less likely to hear about. In fact, the spectacular good decision made under pressure probably would have been unnecessary if a much less urgent decision had been made properly at an earlier stage. It's just like a drive in your car: poor planning or starting a journey too late makes you rush and take unnecessary chances.

Slow down; you may be missing something important!

There is nothing wrong with saying you do not know the answer to a problem or that you don't understand and need time to think. Don't lead other people to expect that you will make a brilliant decision or take action when you don't feel prepared. That just adds pressure, and you have enough of that already.

Tool No. 3: Know the Target

A winner knows never to get into an argument without knowing what he wants to win. He knows that happiness is having what he wants, and he knows what it is that he does want. He knows which offer he will accept and which he will refuse. He knows that if he is without a target he will waste his time and energy. He also knows that his results, no matter how spectacular, are unlikely to make him happy if he is unsure of what he wants.

Tool No. 4: Listen and Watch

If you listen and observe them carefully, other people will tell you almost everything you want or need to know for you to make enlightened decisions. Even though people are often inconsistent, they do reveal themselves in time; but first you have to know how to listen.

For example, if you are buying a house and notice that the seller suddenly seems anxious when he gets to the living room, begin to look around more carefully. See if you can tell where he is looking. If there is a crack running across the ceiling, the seller will probably be staring at it much of the time, drawn to it irresistibly, even if he's trying to look away.

Tool No. 5: Let the Other Guy Worry

Most people, when they sense that another person is anxious, try to put him at ease. Anxiety makes most people uncomfortable. But if you can learn to allow the other person to be anxious and then wait a while, you may discover something important that you would otherwise have missed. If you stay in the living room, the seller will get more nervous and will probably blurt out the fact that the ceiling is unsound and the beams aren't holding the way they should. You will save a fortune just because you let the seller's guilt work on him. Let the person who would trick you give himself away.

Most people are lousy at keeping secrets and assume that others will not pry into their problems. Secretly, they dread that they will be discovered. Given enough opportunity, they confess or give themselves away. Often people are not discovered because others cover up for them out of embarrassment or to avoid making a scene.

Tool No. 6: Silence

When in doubt, Keep Your Mouth Shut.

Working harder is not always the way to make certain that you win in the end. The way to insure winning is to know what you want to win, to understand the tools involved, and to be able to isolate long-term goals from the momentary events in your life. That way you can concentrate your energies on what is important.

Isn't it about time you had a plan for winning and for keeping what you win?

WINNING OFTEN MAKES people feel very uneasy. They regard it as selfish or a way of imposing their will on others. They think winning is mostly bullying and assume that every winner makes someone else a loser. This is usually untrue. Those who win are generally more helpful than losers.

Don't feel guilty about becoming a winner. Winners are the backbone of civilization. Without them there would be no science, no art, no sports, and little excellence of any kind. The only people on top would be those who beat down their fellow man—people like that man who lives in the cave next door and always clubs you as soon as you turn your back to go out hunting mammoths.

Such people are not really winners. They are despots, psychopaths, and bullies who win only because you don't know how to stop them. They win not through any greatness in themselves but because they know how to use your weaknesses, your fear, your uncertainty, your cowardice. Your winning depends on knowing how to handle them, not just on how to handle yourself. Winners are the most desirable citizens because they are best equipped to help others.

If people tend to see winning in a disparaging light it is often because of the way they were brought up. Every mother who has watched her children play has seen their selfishness and cruelty, and she has probably reacted to it.

EIGHT-YEAR-OLD: You took my pencils!

TEN-YEAR-OLD: Liar! They're mine! Ouch! You pinched!

MOTHER: Give them back! You should learn to share, even if they *are* yours.

TEN-YEAR-OLD: She left them out last time. (*Hits eight-year-old sister.*)

MOTHER: What is this, a jungle?

EIGHT-YEAR-OLD: I want them!

MOTHER: Give them back, you're a *big* girl! Start acting decently!

The lesson being taught by this mother is that being grown up means being nice to people even if they're sometimes wrong. Although you are first taught this lesson at home in the hope that members of the same family don't end up killing each other, and to insure some semblance of peace and quiet in the house, you soon begin to apply this sense of fair play in the world outside.

In principle there is nothing wrong with applying this rule, to the outside world, (to be kind, to share, to follow the golden rule) except that it is often misinterpreted or unrealistic. A natural sense of rivalry develops in children as a result of competing for supplies to fill their needs. It's a shame, but it's also a reality: supplies are often limited. Who *will* get the last piece of cake? Who *is* the favorite child? Who *is* the brightest, the prettiest? Who *is* going to get the most money for his education? All through these years of competition most parents struggle to be fair and to referee their children's insatiable drive to be number one in every way within the family.

Parents handle their children by whatever tactic seems to work. They know they should be fair, that "children are only children." Nevertheless, parents become angry and frustrated when they see their children asserting themselves by being nasty, possessive, or cruel to each other, even when such treatment may be warranted. In part, the parent is angry at the child for being unfair and a bully. The parent may also remember feeling cheated by other bullies in life and may act as if the child symbolizes them all.

FATHER: That did it! I will *not* have you punching your brother and calling him names!

SON: He ruined my bicycle!

FATHER: Just who do you think you are, bullying people around like that? You're showing your true colors. Other people have rights!

SON: Well, he ruined my bike just because I beat him in a race!

FATHER: I saw you try to cut him off, you weren't fair! You didn't give him a chance to win.

That's the lesson you learn at home: give everybody a fair chance and share with others even if they don't always deserve it; be big about it. At the same time, beneath the surface, you still feel a strong drive to win, to come out on top, to be number one, to have all of the pie for yourself. But as an adult it makes you feel guilty. When you want so much for yourself, half-forgotten memories return. You may remember a parent who didn't seem to love you so much when you took a toy away from your brother. You felt uncomfortable then. You still do. You were told to be fair all the time and you still believe it down deep somewhere; even now, long after you've discovered that the world is not fair at all.

The drive that propels you to grab the last piece of candy is the same drive that moves you to the head of the class. So it's not surprising that you are always more or less in a turmoil trying to find the balance between succeeding in what you want and pleasing your parents by not being a bully. It's a hard lesson to master. But it's a fact: selfishness appears to be the normal state of human beings. To pretend that it is not is to be unrealistic and, therefore, to be more or less constantly torn between desires.

A human being comes into the world in a totally narcissistic state, a state of complete self-involvement and self-concern. It is normal to want to be selfish. There is very little you can do to stop wanting to be selfish. You can stop *acting* selfish, but the wish to have that last piece of candy, to be number one, to take care of your own needs first, will linger long after you have learned socially acceptable forms of behavior. To pretend that you do not want to be selfish is to run the risk of ruin.

Go On: Be Selfish!

There is no need to pretend you are not selfish; everyone is. The problem is to cope with that selfishness and not feel guilty about it, not go to unnecessary extremes to prove it does not exist.

Young ministers face this hurdle during their training. They often feel ashamed of their selfishness and try to hide it by showing how altruistic they are. Being altruistic, they feel, is more in keeping with "being called." It is only when the ministers accept themselves that they can grow. *You have to admit what you are in order to win.*

In the early years of school, children are hesitant to vote for themselves in class elections. They know that the loser's feelings will be hurt and they have been taught not to hurt other children's feelings. That *was* the parental lesson, remember? Now they must decide whether to vote for themselves or for the kid in the next row. A dilemma! If the child votes for himself, he feels he is being selfish. He knows that only one person can win. He wants to win but doesn't want to make the other child lose. If he loses, he lets himself down. But he did that before, every time he gave up a toy or a turn to his younger brother just to be nice, just to avoid hurting his brother's feelings. He gives in and votes for the other kid and loses by one vote.

To his surprise, his parents seem upset when he tells them the story.

MOTHER: Why'd you do a thing like that? You should've voted for yourself. Don't you want to get ahead?

KID: I dunno.

FATHER: If you're not for yourself, who do you think *will* be?

KID: I dunno. (*Reaches for last potato.*)

MOTHER (*slapping his hand*): You could show some good manners and ask if anyone else would like some potatoes. Offer some to your brother first.

So you enter the outside world unsure of how to get your way without hurting others. The first concept of winning you learn implies that someone else must lose. In some situations there *can* be only one winner; everyone else does lose, as in sports. But in most cases people can win more than they think without defeating anyone else.

You can learn new attitudes about winning. Guilt is usually the result of anger. If winning to you means beating someone and directing your anger at them, you may feel a good deal of guilt as a result. If you don't control your anger, you may end up losing in the long run.

People often describe winning over someone with phrases like, "that got him," "that did him in," "that took him down a peg," or "that beat him into the ground." People tend to see winning over an adversary in physical terms. Thinking about winning in this way may make such people feel particularly guilty about their success, and so their victories are often spoiled.

Although we are taught in childhood to be fair for fairness' sake, that lesson is not widely practiced. Even brothers and sisters with whom you grew up may not be fair. In the end, for all the teaching of parents, children are often remarkably for themselves. This does not mean that brothers and sisters do not help each other if they get into difficulty. Most do. But you don't share everything you own with your brothers and sisters in the same way you were asked to as a child. If you came from a poor family and struck it rich, you might make your poor relatives comfortable in their own eyes, even rich, but you probably wouldn't give them an equal share.

Why not? Well, first of all, you might say you have *your family to think about*. Just look at that statement for a moment. *Your family to think about*. Your wife and kids. That really means you have *you* to think about. Isn't that interesting? To say that you're not sharing for your *family's* sake makes it all right to be selfish. To justify winning and to keep from feeling guilty, some people pretend that they are not winning for themselves.

Why Should You Share?

If you felt more secure, the reason you might give for not sharing is that you earned your success by your own hard work. You *deserve* it. You may feel that your siblings should go out and earn their own way, the way you did.

People who don't win think that you shouldn't keep success to yourself. You should share your good fortune and good luck with them. Everyone is familiar with comments that reflect this attitude ("Now that you're successful, you'll probably forget all your old friends"). To remember your old friends means to share part of your success with them, and sometimes this is appropriate. Those who were friendly with you before you were successful can usually find reasons why they should be included in your success. They often recount advice and ideas that they believe contributed significantly to your success. The fact that you may have been working day and night at an idea for years, or trying to improve yourself, is not nearly so important to them as their belief that you got a "big break." Just your luck!

One of the unfortunate aspects of winning is that others rarely give you credit for doing your share. Luck does play a small part. However, to move at the right opportunity takes knowing that you want to move and that you are ready for it. That's not luck, and the friends who come bearing sour grapes don't know what they're talking about.

Some of the greatest human triumphs result from overcoming a personal hardship and involve an internal struggle from darkness to the light. The music Beethoven composed while he was growing deaf is an example. Winning by confronting and overcoming one's personal problems and hardships is free from the guilt that frequently comes with defeating other people.

The greatest successes are those of an individual triumphing over himself and symbolically conquering the weaknesses common to other men. The successful person concerns himself with his own faults and his own shortcomings and, to himself at least, he does not pretend that he is without blame. He accepts the reality of his limitations and tries to improve. He knows his weaknesses even if to others he appears confident, assured, and all-knowing. He keeps his doubts private, no matter how much disquiet they give him.

Those who win by overcoming their own deficiencies and handicaps have already shared with others by providing inspiration and often by creating works of great humanitarian worth. *Winning means excelling at being you, not hurting other people or using them.* Nevertheless, you must learn how to manage the other people in your life, especially the losers, so that they will not inflict their losing ways on you.

Yes, You Must Manage Other People

No matter how much trouble other people may give you, if you do not succeed it is rarely their fault. More likely you did not know how to manage them. Some would-be winners allow others to ruin their chances for success to avoid testing themselves and to escape being branded as failures. No matter where you go, you can always find others waiting to mess in your affairs and screw up your work. It is naive to expect that you will succeed merely because you know what to do and how to do it. If you want to win, you must take others into consideration and manage them.

When you manage other people, *you aren't manipulating them as much as you are helping them.* Remember: people who succeed are usually aware of their own failures and they struggle to overcome them. Losers attempt to blame the rest of the world for their mistakes. They also like to make things go wrong for others so that they themselves look better. In the process of getting a loser out of your way you may help him to get out of his own.

You do not spare a loser by not asserting yourself. You only allow him to postpone the inevitable day when he will fall down. By going along with losers you only perpetuate their belief that the fault is in the world around them, not within themselves. People are hesitant about confronting losers with the facts or showing them how they mess everything up, because they feel embarrassed for them, and uncomfortable because they are relieved that it's not their fault.

A waitress breaks stacks of plates in the kitchen and gets away with it because the cook is a kindly warm man who can't bear to see someone else look sad. The cook says, "Don't worry, everyone makes mistakes." So the waitress is not told that she piled the dishes too high.

Losers have a penchant for being lazy, which they try to disguise and present as cutting corners and saving steps and effort, time and money. They try to justify their laziness as doing you a favor. The waitress will tell the cook that she was only being more efficient in his poorly run kitchen.

See? It's the cook's fault for running such a disorganized, inefficient kitchen that the waitress had to pile the dishes up. As a result of the cook's good nature, *no problem has been discussed.* The waitress will do it again. You can bet on it. Again the cook will not correct her. So the cook will be upset and start to make mistakes and will ruin a large preparation of food. And the waitress, who thinks it's everyone else's fault, will point out the cook's mistake to the manager as proof of an inefficiently run kitchen.

Losers lose the most when they are allowed to get away with mistakes. They only get more deeply entrenched in their losing ways.

So don't feel guilty about being a winner! The ones who should feel guilty are the losers, and they're too busy trying to find fault with everyone else. When a loser begins to set you up as his patsy, point it out to him as soon as possible. Losers spend their lives trying to get other people to adopt their problems and to accept responsibility for them. The only way to handle losers is to get them out of your way and act to win.

IF YOU DON'T have a plan, it's almost impossible to win. Why make it any more difficult for yourself? There's a lot you already know about winning. What you don't know is how to put it all together to make an effective plan of attack. So let's go over some basic points. Don't scoff at these ideas and say, "I already know this." Of course you do, but can you put this information to use? Can you keep all these points in mind when it counts? You've got to if you want to win.

Rule No. 1: Be Selective

Nobody can win at everything and nobody can win all the time. In fact, there are times when you definitely would not want to win, when winning would be the worst possible tactic because it would make you lose in the long run.

Rule No. 2: Pick Your Opponent

A businessman should not try to beat a prospective client at golf; it would be an expensive and perhaps disastrous victory. Although it might offend a competitive client if you don't make an effort to win, it's a rare client who enjoys being beaten. Everyone likes to be on top, but certain people, especially bigwigs, bosses, etc., feel they *must* be. Recognize who they are and try to let them feel they have their way.

Rule No. 3: Pick Your Point

This may seem manipulative and crafty, but it really is not. You wouldn't be playing golf with a prospective client if you really wanted a PGA quality game would you? You are entertaining the client, letting him win, just as you let your three year-old win when you play together. The game you are really playing is to win the account. That is the game that counts. Don't confuse major and minor points.

Rule No. 4: Let Others Help You

You can't take charge of every situation in your life and you should allow others to assume responsibility even if you feel you could do it better. Not to delegate responsibility just wastes time. The housewife who hates the way her kids make the beds and therefore makes them herself, who washes the dishes because she's better at that, too, and picks up after them, may find that she does not have any time left to take the night courses she planned. If she could lower some of her standards she could delegate some responsibility to the kids. They're old enough and willing. To have all the little details go her way she may end up losing in the end, not getting the graduate degree she wants.

Rule No. 5: Make a Plan

If you intend to win, start planning. Develop your skills. Enhance your ability. Focus on activities you like best and find most natural to do. That's probably where your talent lies. People who have never·done this often reach a plateau in their lives where they feel trapped and unable to advance. Although they are good at what they do, they are often dissatisfied because they belong elsewhere but never planned effectively how to get there.

I know a lawyer who, in spite of achieving considerable financial success and a brilliant reputation among his colleagues, felt empty to the point of desolation much of the time. He always wanted to be a sculptor. During law school he managed to take courses and even sold a few works. He planned to sculpt and live off a small law practice. As his law practice grew, his time became scarcer. He gave in to family pressures and abandoned his sculpting. Because he had no guide to follow, he lost his way.

Now he is nearing forty and can't stand living with himself. Although he is brilliant and well-trained, he firmly believes that what he does in law is not really special, that anyone who tried equally hard could do as well. He enjoys no emotional reward from his practice and feels as if his entire life is wasted. Even though in the eyes of those who know him he looks like a winner, he is the world's biggest loser where it counts most—in his own eyes. It is difficult to overstate how unhappy he feels about himself. That unhappiness was compounded by other people because they failed to find anything tragic about him. They resented him and thought his protestations and sadness were childish.

So, to make sure you have a chance to win, you must be sure to choose the goal you really want to attain.

Rule No. 6: Expect a Bill

The idea that nothing is free still sounds like news to some people. Everything you do (or receive) costs something. Eventually you will have to pay the price. Successful people know and accept this. They don't try to avoid paying. Losers are just the opposite.

If successful people always pay, why are they the ones who enjoy themselves, who have more leisure time, more respect, yet seem to pay so little, whether the price is money, leisure time, emotional upset, or inconvenience?

Successful people do pay for their success, but their timing is better and their terms seem more favorable to them.

When you know what you want, you should find out what it will cost and what the currency consists of. You should pay as soon as possible. And if you understand that nobody gets away without paying for what he receives and you can accept this, you have already won half the battle.

Suppose you want to succeed as a musician. Your currency is practice. Nothing else will help you make the grade. Even if you have a great deal of talent you must still work at becoming a success.

Winners accept the necessity to work very hard even before they begin and fully commit themselves to the task. Consequently, they master the needed skills and progress rapidly, and their early success keeps their interest and morale high.

Others, no less talented, labor under the illusion that talent alone will carry them through the rough spots. They therefore do not work as hard. When their results fall short of their expectations they are disappointed. They may then abandon the field entirely rather than risk further defeat. They usually don't realize that they did not really try. Some even retreat knowing that they did not give their best.

If you have a talent and do not try to use it at some time, you will be unhappy about it. The years are generally not kind to those who postpone unless they need more time to be sure of their goals before they can make their best effort.

The price of everything goes up over the years. When you postpone your search for goals or do not give your best effort, you'll find that each time around it takes more effort. Finally your goal is beyond you. This is how once-possible goals begin to drift away. Then you look at people who have no more talent than you and are doing what you should be doing. They live the kind of life you wanted, and you just feel defeated.

Winning at a career or life style is similar in many ways to trading in stocks. You should buy when the price is low, and sell high. You do best to start pursuing your goal as soon as you are sure about it and to expend as much time and effort as possible when success is easiest to "buy." The daily routines of life soon manage to creep into everyone's plans and take over time and space, leaving little room for growth. As the years pass, fewer resources are available to invest in something new. It is more difficult to revive an old goal, but it still is possible.

Rule No. 7: Do Your Thing

Successful people seem to have more time and energy to do what they want. When you do what you want, your activities become self-actualizing. Your work fulfills you because it is a logical extension of who you are and what you believe. When someone's life reflects his inner self, he is emotionally enriched by what he does. The harder he works, the more enriched he feels, the more energy he has.

Again, it's just like growth stocks. Time invested in the early years produces a sense of accomplishment, self-fulfillment, and energy.

Successful people are often able to identify their best abilities before others are aware of themselves. They play their hunches with everything they have. They specialize and try to do only what they do better than anyone else. Agatha Christie writes mystery stories, not lyrics to popular songs, because that is what she does best. Oversimplified, maybe. But true. Are you doing most what you do best? Why not?

Rule No. 8: Pick Your Time

Winners seem to have mastered the necessary skills when the least investment was required. Most chronic problems could have been more easily resolved when they first came up.

This is especially true with problems of daily living: a problem child, controlling termites, keeping the lawn green during the summer. Let those problems get out of hand and you'll really have trouble. Obvious again? Maybe, but why are there so many problem kids, termite-infested homes, and yellow lawns? Someone is missing his timing.

Rule No. 9: Don't Ignore Mistakes

As soon as you see a situation turn bad or fail to meet expectations, take adequate time to consider all actions that are open to you; that is the best time to correct it. Again, this may sound obvious and simplistic, but it is really fundamental. When a mistake is discovered, a plan should be worked out to prevent further lapses. There's nothing like recognizing that your welfare is in serious danger to make you act effectively. But you must recognize when you are in danger. Many people don't till it's too late.

Rule No. 10: Pick What's Important

This is the basic rule of every discipline that involves action. You must set priorities. In medicine, one is taught first to make sure that an emergency victim can breathe; next, that his heart is functioning. To correct other problems before these two have been remedied is to lose the patient. Medical problems contain a built-in logic that takes into account how important a bodily misfunction is and what the most likely cause is. The goal in medicine is to save the patient. What that requires is usually well known and well ordered.

You need priorities in your life, too. Decide which factors you consider vital to reaching your dreams and goals. Then arrange them in order of importance. Then monitor these functions closely to detect and correct mistakes before they get out of hand.

Rule No. 11: Monitor Your Progress

No matter how closely you keep track of the important variables in your life, like a businessman watching sales, the watching is useless unless you pay attention as soon as progress seems to slow down. If you follow your progress closely, you will be way ahead of the crowd. You'll be much more aware of impending failures and success than other people. You'll know the score before it's final—maybe even long before.

Many people are afraid to look this closely at themselves, and so they miss the earliest warning signs of serious problems. Unfortunately, this is the time when problems are most easily corrected.

You must know which variables to follow. Even if you know your goals, the problem is not simple. Deciding what to monitor requires that you determine what factors your goal depends upon and how you want each to progress. A salesman might monitor the number of new customers, his sales volume, the size of his territory, or the number of calls he makes a day. His boss might follow sales, production, cash flow, and profits.

When nothing is done to correct it, a bad situation almost always gets worse. Don't wait for time to heal a worsening situation. If you don't know what's wrong take the time to find out. Problems that were manageable can suddenly become overwhelming. People may hesitate to correct a problem because they do not recognize it; or are afraid to admit failure; or don't know what to do. Students rely on their grades to tell them how they stand; performers have critics; employees hame promotions. Every goal has its own measurable variables. You must decide which variables to follow and how to read the results.

Rule No. 12: Look for Causes, Not Effects

You can make vastly different decisions based on the same information. It is best to follow causes, rather than effects.

If a company is unable to sell its product even after repeatedly reducing prices, it would be foolish to hire more salesmen. Something is wrong with the product—something that makes it unattractive at almost any price. The product must be changed or abandoned, the way the Ford Motor Company eventually jettisoned the Edsel.

Rule No. 13: Chart Your Future

Choosing what to monitor in your personal life is more complex than choosing in the business world. Begin by listing those qualities that you think you will need or that you would like to have when you finally do arrive at your goal. Next, rank them in order of importance. Finally, when appropriate, set a goal for each variable.

This is a list prepared by a young man aspiring to be president of the company where he is presently assistant sales manager. The list is in *his* order.

> Increase my product knowledge, especially in new products —two new products each week.
> Have more meetings with salesmen; two more per month.
> Learn more about managing people. Attend a seminar on this.
> Develop at least three ways of being personally useful to the president.
> Give the impression of being a member of the company team, daily.
> Find ten new ways of interrelating my sales function with other parts of the company.

This list makes it easier for this man to concentrate his energies. He must still manage the daily responsibilities of his job. But now he has a better chance of acting at the right signal, and more efficiently.

The following list was drawn up by a woman who plans to begin a second career in interior decorating once her youngest baby goes to school. It reflects her unfamiliarity with the field and is an example of an exploratory list.

> Call interior decorators to see how *they* began.
> Call up several interior decorating schools.
> Buy books on the subject and read, read, read.
> Buy a small drawing board and experiment with room layouts.
> Get a background in design and art somewhere.
> Go to interior decorating school or get proper training.

The way one monitors each item on the list varies. "Call interior decorators," etc., means simply to call asking for suggestions. This information should be kept in a small notebook and should become the basis for future lists.

This procedure may be helpful to people who are organized and efficient as well as to those who are not. When you arrange these factors in a list you begin to visualize them and to assert control over them. You can better determine how much energy to expend and in what direction. Also, new possibilities appear. From time to time the list should be rewritten and the priorities reordered as your knowledge about the subject grows. This housewife's list becomes more to the point after she has looked into some of the early possibilities. Here's her list three months later:

> Get a part-time job at the Modern Design Shop for experience.
> Take another course in decorating.
> Do some studying about fabrics.
> Read at least one book about decorating each week.
> Volunteer my services to friends just to get my name known.

Eventually as she develops more skills and feels more sure of herself, her future list will reflect that. It will become more concerned with new ideas, less with technique. Here's her list one year after she got started:

Cultivate customers at Modern Design.
Make myself known to Modern Design's suppliers.
Look for occasional freelance work.
Think about opening my own shop, get facts and figures.

The progression should run from a disorganized, perhaps vague collection of skills and goals in an early list, to a more highly organized arrangement of priorities later on that better reflect your personality.

Rule No. 14: Conserve Your Energy

Success also depends upon knowing how to use your energy. You have to know when to concede minor points in order to save your strength. It's just as important to know when a battle cannot be won and *how to lose* it. Retreating is an art too!

You are playing tennis and are behind, five games to nothing in the first set. But you have just begun to play well. You have several alternatives. First, you could begin to play as hard as possible to win all the remaining games in the set in a row. That would require a tremendous effort. The odds against you are oppressive. You might wear yourself out. You could try to win a game or two, just to make sure that you are really warmed up for the next set, and accept the reality of losing the first set. Then you can try harder and have a better chance in the next set with the intent of winning there. Or you could just not try and lose the first set by a shut-out.

The plan with the best chance of winning is to warm up. It allows for correcting your deficiencies. It also keeps the door open in the event that you can win the first set. But to make an all-out challenge will only drain your energy and may crush your morale so that you will have little left to win in the end.

Rule No. 15: Know When to Lose

Valuable resources are often wasted attempting to correct hopeless situations. Usually, chances for correcting an error grow less likely and more costly the later the hour.

This is the problem faced by inexperienced investors when they hold a very bad stock and don't know how to get out of it. They are afraid to admit defeat and take a loss. So they hold on and watch the stock drop. They discover reasons why the stock should be going up soon or why that company will have a better year next year. While this is going on, many other stocks (in which they could just as well be investing) are going up. Unfortunately, these people use up energy and capital to persuade themselves that they made the right decision, which they didn't. Little energy is available for looking around and analyzing other issues. They have forgotten their goal. Their goal is not to make money on every stock they invest in, or to prove to the world that they are infallible financial wizards. Their goal is to make the most money possible in the long run. They lose by trying too hard to win. Whenever you buy stock you should set a limit: the lowest price to which you will let the stock fall. And when it falls to that price—sell!

It is impossible to go through life with goals as clear cut and variables as measurable as in the stock market, but to live without any effort to set priorities is to waste time and energy and only makes it necessary to invest more later to correct present mistakes. When you have a long-range plan, taking a small loss in a bad stock won't seem like a personal injury or proof of your incompetence, especially if the next investment turns out well.

Rule No. 16: Learn to Deal With Slumps

There are good days and bad days for correcting a situation. Before you act, determine whether events have really gone bad or whether the unfortunate turn is part of the normal cycle through which all human events pass. Baseball players go through slumps; students have dull periods. But remember: there is a danger of using being in a slump as an excuse. If you establish goals and know the variables involved, you will know how to measure performance, so slumps should present only a temporary lag.

Rule No. 17: Use the Secret of Life

A patient had been in a mental hospital for several years waiting to discover the secret of life, which he said would allow him to leave the hospital and be well again. He spent many hours discussing his potential discovery. It was impossible to get him to consider his own role in the circumstances that caused his despair. According to him, his problems were caused by forces outside him. As sometimes happens, he began to believe that his doctor knew the secret of life and that he wasn't getting better because the doctor would not tell him. After much arguing the doctor finally promised to tell him the secret of life.

At the next visit the conversation went something like this:

DOCTOR: I have thought this over very carefully and have decided to keep my promise. But this secret is so upsetting to some people that they refuse to believe it.

PATIENT: I'll believe it, if it's the real secret of life.

DOCTOR: It is. Once you hear it, you'll know because it's very obvious, although most people overlook it.

PATIENT: Tell me!

DOCTOR: The secret of life is . . . that there is no secret of life.

PATIENT: What?

DOCTOR: It's all hard work.

PATIENT: That's no secret! That's a lot of crap!

DOCTOR: Listen for a moment. Look at all the people who are looking for the secret of life. Did you ever meet anyone who found it?

PATIENT: No. No one's found it.

DOCTOR: That's right! You waste your life looking, expecting miracles, and nothing happens. Meanwhile, the people who know that they have to work for what they want begin to get somewhere.

The patient was very upset by this, but did agree to try to test out the new idea. He began to work in the greenhouse, eventually got a job with a florist, and left the hospital.

If you accept the fact that you have to work for success and realize that the amount of work diminishes rapidly once the first investment has been made, you understand the principle exactly. The idea of facing hard work is unpleasant to many people because *they see it as an endless cycle leading nowhere*. Indeed, if their energy is invested in a search after the wrong goals (or the wrong part of the right goals) they may not succeed. Then the cycle *does* lead nowhere and *is* endless.

Remember: you have a limited amount of time and energy. In order to succeed, you must choose your long-range goals carefully; isolate the various components of each of the goals; and work as hard as possible to fulfill them. It's very much like learning a language. The more attention you give to mastering grammar and vocabulary in the beginning, the easier it becomes later on. When this is not done, the task looks hopelessly difficult and you waste time catching up, forever trying to correct mistakes you made earlier.

WHILE IT IS TRUE that nothing succeeds like success, nothing helps success as much as clear vision.

A winner is usually able to answer the question "What do you want?" in a way that is meaningful to him. This does not mean that he will always have a specific answer that is meaningful to other people. An artist may answer, "Perfection," and know what he means. The artist may be searching for his particular kind of truth, and while he may not have the ability to define that goal, he can recognize what is not true and reject it.

The self-made very rich knew at the beginning that they wanted to be very rich. They wasted little time on activities that did not hold the promise of helping to make them very rich. Successful people are able to focus sharply on their needs and energetically seek answers to fulfill those needs as closely as possible. Their self-awareness allows them to identify quickly whatever situations are vital to their goals and, as I have emphasized, they act on these situations as soon as they recognize them and do so with a full sense of commitment.

This is not to say that great successes understand everything that motivates them. Indeed, if they did, many of them would probably be less effective. Rather, winners understand what they need to be happy *in their own terms*. They know what compromises are unimportant and are willing to make them. They also know when they must stand fast.

Don't Ignore the Bad Apple

Besides knowing who he is and what it will take to win, the winner also knows what threatens his chances and can make him lose. He has a clear picture of the bad apple that will ruin the entire barrel. Much of his thinking is directed to finding this bad apple and getting rid of it. This is what a boss does when he gets rid of an employee who undermines morale. No winner ever ignores potential contaminants. This is just as important as knowing what it takes to win.

The winner also possesses a strong sense of personal integrity. He knows what is his and what is not, *where the boundaries of his own rights begin and end.* This feeling for what is appropriate applies to everything he thinks and does, at least much of the time. He knows which problems are his and which are caused by other people; he doesn't blame his salesman if his product is faulty. He knows which of the other people's problems he will have to shoulder and solve in order to succeed and which he can leave to the other fellow. If a sale is very important and the salesman can't sell, he makes the sale himself. But he knows how to stick to his own business. He knows what he is responsible for, yet he is not reluctant to help others if that's what it takes to win. He doesn't feel guilty about succeeding.

Even though people usually dislike being reminded that they are not so distantly related to animals, the establishment of territorial limits is one of the most basic laws of animal and human life. After birds establish their nests they announce that fact, often with special territorial calls. When a strange bird violates the established territory, he is invariably challenged the moment the violation is noted. If the limits are not established and the stranger is not challenged, the stranger is free to take over.

Why You Must Assert Your Rights

Our own civil law is based on a similar code. If you do not protect your property sufficiently, you may lose your claim to it. If your neighbors use a foot path that crosses your yard and you never point out that they are on private property, they may eventually establish a right of way, and you will run the risk of losing title to the path. Some states rule that after a certain number of years of failure to protect ownership, the right of way falls into the public domain. To prevent this, the owner must block off the path one day a year to indicate that it is private property, an act as symbolic as the birds' call.

Failure to assert one's rights can result in the loss of a valuable trademark. The name "cellophane" was once owned by the company that first made the product. As similar products appeared on the market the name cellophane became descriptive of the material in general and was no longer thought of as a brand name. Because the owners of the name were not aggressive enough in defending their sole right to use it, they lost that right.

Interestingly enough, the law states that as soon as you become aware that your rights have been violated you are bound to act to protect them as soon as you can. If you don't, you will lose them. If this sounds a good deal like the birds protecting their nests against invaders, it is meant to—because it is. You keep what you own because you are willing to protect it.

The world is not entirely ruled by the law of the jungle; to go through life suspiciously keeping vigil would be unbearable. But life would be even worse if you allowed others to do whatever they want with what you own. You'd end up with nothing. You have to decide what you wish to protect, and protect it!

The successful person is always aware of his territorial rights and is willing to defend them. When someone is taking what is his (be it his property, his turn, or his time), he knows it. He responds rapidly to infringements, before others have a chance to establish claims on what is his, and when the effort to do so is minimal. He knows: the longer he waits, the weaker his case becomes.

Yes, the asserting of territorial rights refers not only to property but also to intangibles, such as your place in line at the supermarket, or your right to a parking space when you get there first, or the right to peace and quiet in your life.

Imagine that you are watching a movie. Behind you some people are extremely noisy and ruining your evening. If you feel uncomfortable about telling them to shut up and you can find another seat, you have found one solution. If you don't find another seat, you must ask them to be quiet or they will feel they have earned the right to be noisy merely because you have accepted that fact. If you don't complain until you're angry, you will be argumentative and will be less effective in dealing with them because you will be causing the same problem as they were—making noise and disturbing others.

Fight Only the Important Battles

While a winner will not tolerate people taking advantage of him, he realizes he cannot correct every inequity in life. So he commits himself fully to battle only when he knows he can achieve some relief. He saves his energy for the important struggles.

Let's assume that you have asked the people behind you in the movie to be quiet, but they refuse to cooperate; perhaps they have been drinking and are acting belligerently. There are no other seats. You *do* want to see that movie. It is quite difficult for you to act with authority because you appear to be no different from anyone else to these noisy people. You must speak to the manager and insist that he act at once. It's true you may miss a few scenes in the movie while you speak with him, but it is better than trying to see the entire show and not enjoying any of it because you are so preoccupied with anger. Besides, the manager *will* be seen as an authority by the noisy patrons, and he is accustomed to dealing with people like this. Be very firm and polite with him and make it clear that you aren't going to put up with the situation.

You do well to make your feelings known even if you're going to lose. You'll feel better, and for good reason. If you do not express anger when a person injures you, that anger gets bottled up inside and struggles to get out. Angry fantasies expand if they are not expressed, sometimes so strongly that they leave little room to think about anything else. Winners don't put up with such emotional ballast.

So if someone hurts you, tell them that they are hurting you and that you don't like it. Most people are afraid to speak up that way. As a result, the people who hurt them go right on hurting them. Most people are not malicious. Most hurts are unintentional, so if offenders had been informed at once they probably would have stopped. But time has a peculiar way of altering attitudes. The longer you delay in telling someone that he is hurting you, the less believable your complaint appears when you finally reveal it. You must speak up to protect your emotional right of way!

Go Ahead: Complain!

Imagine you pay a kid to mow your lawn and trim the beds. Then you discover that he doesn't weed the way you like. You don't complain even though you feel irritated. After the place looks like a hay field you do complain to him. He thinks you're unfair and should pay him extra to do what you request. You get outraged and fire the kid. This leaves you with (1) an unweeded lawn; (2) a hatred for the kid and, maybe, for all kids; (3) anger at yourself for having handled the situation like a loser; and (4) the need to find another kid—who may do an even worse job.

The person who has been hurting you establishes a routine and in time becomes used to it. It becomes an accepted way of life since you never objected before. Asking this kid to give up his routine will be felt by him as a loss. Now the injured party and the injuring party seem to reverse roles. The chance for settlement of differences diminishes, especially since by now the problem has grown to uncontrollable proportions.

This principle can be applied throughout life. Again: *if someone hurts you, tell him.* If he is wrong and you can make him see your side of the situation, he is very likely to change and act more acceptably. He will probably be embarrassed and feel a bit guilty about his selfish actions and may even be glad you told him. Asserting your rights is not taking advantage of other people, but you must do so quickly and without over-reacting. You don't need to stand up in the movie and scream. Let the manager over-react if he so chooses. The very nature of being human requires people to act as check-and-balance systems against each other. The time to cry out is when you are injured.

Let's look at a simple incident and see how responses vary when you wait to report an infringement on your rights.

A group of friends are at the beach.

VERSION ONE: PROTEST NOW AND TELL WHY

STAN: You stepped on my camera!

BILL: I'm sorry. I'll be more careful. Is it okay?

STAN: I guess it'll be okay, but let's look at it. No, the shutter's jammed.

BILL: I'm sorry. I'll take care of the damage, Stan.

In this episode Bill is made aware of his action. Stan also mentions what seems wrong with the camera. Stan has the best chance of winning compensation for his damages because Bill cannot deny his part.

VERSION TWO: PROTEST NOW, BUT
DON'T TELL WHY TILL LATER

STAN: Hey! Watch it!

BILL: Whoops!

In this version Stan might collect for the damages, but he has to do a lot more convincing that the camera was broken by that specific act of Bill's, not by another person. The incident is vague to Bill, not firmly anchored in his mind.

VERSION THREE: POSTPONE EVERYTHING

BILL *steps on* STAN'S *camera and neither comments.*

In this version Bill may have no recollection of the event at all. Remember that events that make you feel guilty are the ones you tend to repress, to push away. Stan has become angry but can't bring himself to tell Bill about the incident until he discovers how much the repairs cost. Now it's several days later.

STAN: Boy, that's just the way you are! No respect for anyone else's property! You're just thinking of you all the time! Ruining my camera!!

BILL: I don't know what you're talking about! What's got into you! I never touched your camera!

STAN: You broke my camera because you were inconsiderate!

BILL: Why are you trying to blame your problems on me?

Stan lost his temper and presented his case inappropriately by attacking Bill's personality. He made the situation seem ridiculous to Bill, who barely remembers it and now believes that he had no part in it to begin with. Bill doesn't think of himself as inconsiderate or disrespectful of other people's property. These accusations are the product of Stan's buried anger, which has caused him to distort the facts. Bill may know that he stepped on the camera but now feels more comfortable denying everything. Stan's anger made Bill less willing to own up. To admit now that he damaged the camera would make him seem to agree with all of the other accusations Stan has made.

To win in a battle over personal rights one should stick with the facts of the injury and not delve into motivations or personalities. Let the other person's guilt take care of that. In time it will. Just list the damages and the nature of the infringement, and do it quickly.

That's the law of nature and of civilization. To be a winner, you have to live by it. To re-emphasize: this does not mean that you should take advantage of others and violate their territorial limits. Nothing could be more injurious to your own success. Robert Frost is right: *good fences do make good neighbors.* Moral philosophers may debate the nature of man, his intentions, and his "meanness," but here it is only useful to point out that in daily interactions between people, those who get along best know what is theirs and what is their neighbors'; and when they defend what is their own, their neighbors respect their claims to it.

As mentioned before, to be a success often requires little more than avoiding failure. When you let people take advantage of you, you not only lose the ability to assert yourself, you also weaken the habit of standing up for and keeping what is yours. This does not mean that one cannot be generous. *One should be generous, but by intention, not by default.* If you so tax yourself by giving in to others that you are unable to generate the resources you need to be truly generous, everyone suffers. You must know your own limits. Living beyond your energy (or emotional or financial limits) eventually takes its toll.

What If You Do Damage?

What should you do when you hurt someone? It is really impossible to avoid paying for the damage that we do to others.

The best way to handle this is simply to concede the damage in general terms. The other party, who often will be very angry, will not be expecting your admission of guilt and will probably be more lenient than otherwise.

HE: You drove your car right into mine!

SHE: The bumper is scratched. I'm sorry. (*This is a general statement that admits a fact.*)

HE: It sure is! You should have looked where you were going!

SHE: There's some damage to my car too. (*This is a good idea! Indicate you've been hurt, too. It takes the sting out of your adversary's anger.*)

HE: Women drivers should be taken off the road!

SHE: What other damage did I do? (*Another good point: ignore hostile comments.*)

HE: This nick here, boy! And here's another one!

SHE: I'm sorry! The car must have started to roll without my noticing it. I did nick it. (*Good! Admit it again. This makes the argument less heated.*)

HE: Yeah, must have!

In any accident the principally injured party needs time to let his anger out. The feeling exists, and it has to go somewhere. Don't offer a lame or transparent excuse. It will just be an extra-juicy target for all that anger. People who are hit in an accident often react to it as if it had been a personal attack on them. They need to be reassured that it was not. They also need to know enough fresh information from the other person to allow them to identify with him and thereby to view him as human ("It could happen to anybody"). Telling the other driver that the car rolled turns the accident into a situation that the injured driver might recognize from his own experience.

So if you've injured another person, don't start denying it. Allow room for the anger to blow off and don't take it personally. If you do, this will only botch up everything and push you deeper into needless controversy. Let the other person express his anger while you remain quiet, or just agree that the damage has taken place. In a while the anger will subside. Since the anger will be much greater than called for in most cases, the other party may start to feel self-conscious about being so angry. After all, it *was* an accident and he realizes it. You didn't intend to hurt him. You're just trying to be decent about it and make the best of it.

The lesson of personal (and especially territorial) rights is one of the most important to master to become a winner. Although most threats to your territorial rights seem to come from the outside (someone is always ready to take over what's yours), those who threaten you see your failure to set the goals and limits for yourself as an invitation to intrude. Winners view the violation of their territory as their own fault. They have as sharp an eye on their own weaknesses as they do on others. They know if anyone is to blame for their failure it is probably themselves.

ALTHOUGH IN MANY SITUATIONS losers merely act in ways that are opposite to those of winners, losers are sufficiently distinctive to deserve a chapter of their own. Losing is a virulent and contagious disease. It makes everyone miserable who becomes exposed to it. A loser's symptoms include feelings of long-standing discontent with the world and a need to blame others for his own problems, often associated with a tendency to denigrate others. His misery leads to the belief, often fixed, that very few of life's joys are really worth his effort to obtain them.

As the disease becomes chronic, the loser characteristically withdraws and avoids new activities that might give pleasure. Enjoyment of situations that once were pleasurable begins to diminish. Everything seems the same—bland and colorless. Often the loser cannot distinguish between special ways and ordinary ways of doing anything—cooking, painting, decorating, or working. This is a typical defense of losers for saving their own face and preserving their faltering self-image. Since everything gradually appears gray and uninteresting, they find little difference between their performance and the performance of winners. Ultimately, losing is a loss of the ability to love oneself and a tendency to blame the world for that loss.

Losers characteristically act very late, often only when a situation has deteriorated beyond their ability to cope with it.

Even though they lose frequently enough, losers lose even further because they do not know how to lose. They continue fighting in vain until their resources have been seriously depleted and their ability to recover their losses in another venture is greatly compromised. Their poorly managed defeats insure future defeats.

Losers like a lot of company because they dislike feeling unique; nobody wants to be the only failure in his neighborhood. Losers also spend much of their time looking for excuses: the examination was too hard, the team lost the game because of a rotten break, the boss was picking on them. They need company to bolster their fallen self-image. They are more interested in justifying failure than in correcting it. If you spend any time with losers you might hear conversations like the following.

BUCKY: Boy, the boss sure screwed me by making me work Saturday, don't you think?

PAUL: We all have to take turns. I took mine.

BUCKY: Al has never worked on a Saturday. Al hasn't taken a turn.

PAUL: He hasn't?

BUCKY: See, you didn't know! You're lucky that I told you. The boss is screwing you too.

Before Paul knows it, Bucky will give him all the excuses he'll need so he'll feel picked on and resentful for not getting his share. That's how losers work. They give you reasons outside yourself to explain why you're not successful (the same ones they rely on). If Paul agrees with Bucky, and it's tempting to do so, he feels better about his own failures. The boss becomes Paul's culprit, too. Now that Paul is angry at the boss he shows it by doing poor work. He stops advancing. He feels, "What's the use? I can work hard and nothing will happen. The boss isn't fair!"

Losing is a self-fulfilling prophesy.

Losing is often the result of taking the easy way out (just as Paul is doing.) There is a time to lose in order to win later on. Chess players sacrifice pieces for a better position on the board. Sometimes one gives up holidays at work in order to wind up with a better job in the end. When losing appears to be winning, it is probably a short-term solution to a long-term problem (like a long-distance runner leading the field but losing in the end).

Never Join Forces With a Loser!

When you are trying to get ahead and meet a loser obstructing you, you discover that you argue from different points of view. Losers see the struggle as existing between them and other people, not within themselves. Thus they strive to put you down. Being aware of this can help you manage them. In your early struggle to win, you are most vulnerable and may seek the company of others for the safety of belonging to a group. But don't let losers include you in their failures!

In order to prevent this interference, you need to know as much about losers as about winners. If you don't watch out, they'll end up blaming you. Imagine if Bucky had convinced Paul that they should approach the boss together. The conversation between the three of them would have gone like this:

BUCKY: He (*meaning Paul*) and I feel that we've been taken advantage of because Al has never worked on Saturday.

BOSS: Oh? Come to think of it, Bucky, neither have you until this week. Al is scheduled for the following week. (*To Paul*) I thought you needed the money, Paul. I was thinking of moving you up.

Paul allowed himself to fall into Bucky's trap and the boss associated him with Bucky. Paul is a decent worker. Bucky crabs the very first time he is asked to do something. Paul would have done better to act differently, to stand alone when Bucky first started his crabbing:

BUCKY: Boy, the boss is sure screwing us by making us work Saturdays.

PAUL: He pays us overtime for it.

BUCKY: You gonna take being treated like that?

PAUL: I like my job.

BUCKY: No one's got a right to ask you to work Saturday!

PAUL: He's the boss. I need the extra work. If you don't like it, quit.

BUCKY: I'm gonna protest to the union rep. What are you, a company man?

PAUL: I'm a . . .

WAIT! Don't say another word, Paul! Just go back to work. Think about it. In a minute Bucky will start dealing with you as if you were the boss and he'll push you to the point where you have to make some kind of comment against the company just to show that you're a good guy and on the employees' side. Like, maybe, "I couldn't give a good goddam about this company. I'm just thinking of my future."

Before you know what happens, Bucky will go to the boss and say, "Paul says that he couldn't give a good goddam about the company if you make us work overtime. I don't want to sound rash, boss, but some of the other men in the shop feel the same way." Given the opportunity, Bucky will put words in your mouth. Believe it: losing is a contagious disease.

Because their self-image is insufficient to make them feel confident without reassurances from outside themselves, losers are too much concerned with the opinions of others. They may act to please others by fulfilling what they imagine are the others' expectations. The loser loses the most when he acts to preserve principles he does not believe in or understand (like not admitting when he's wrong, just to save face). Nations can be notorious losers when they get into such a bind. Our Vietnam war policy is an example. Not knowing when to lose, we nearly ruined our country for the sake of appearances.

Losers often don't realize they will lose and are therefore unprepared to face reversals. When the time comes that you must lose, it's best to do so gracefully and as soon as possible. This allows you to reorganize your thoughts and opens up routes to future victories by gathering the remaining forces together for another winning day.

Losers often do not recognize themselves as independent individuals but rather think of themselves as hovering closely attached to other people on whom they sometimes try to blame their failures. They tend to disown what is bad in themselves and appropriate what is good in others. When their rights are violated they are uncertain about how to protect them. Winners know themselves without reference to others; losers frequently need to refer to others to make a statement about themselves. It is rare for a loser to say, "I am good." It is more common to hear, "I am as good as anyone," or "I am as good as the next fellow."

Whose Fault Is It, Anyway?

The loser does not set standards for himself that help him toward success, even though he seems to try. He is often competitive, but in the very worst sense of the word. All he wants is not to be last. Losers, like winners, rarely enjoy losing. But unlike winners, they refuse to recognize that their failure is their fault. Winners accept the fact that they are sometimes inept, but they only see this as proof that they are human. They do not feel the need to waste time explaining it. Because losers cannot accept failure as part of themselves they do not profit from their mistakes.

This talent for being a killjoy is partly caused by the losers' low self-esteem. If losers cannot accept responsibility for their own failures, they may have difficulty accepting responsibility for their own success. Losers may point to their successes as proof that they are worthwhile persons. If one looks more closely, it is clear that they really believe they have been very lucky, even deserving, but not responsible for their victory. How could they then explain their failures? So even when a loser wins, he still feels like a loser. Secretly believing that what has happened to him is the result of luck, he cannot trust it and cannot accept and enjoy it. A loser can understand winning at a lottery, but winning by struggling over the years seems like too much work to him. Besides, he suspects it is evanescent and can disappear like the morning mist.

Because he is unable to accept his infrequent success, he rarely feels secure; the loser is always a child of "fortune," good or bad.

Since the loser's standards are vague, he or she may be unaware of threats. What if a housewife doesn't recognize that her husband's three-martini lunches are actually symptoms of alcoholism? By the time she understands what is happening to him, it is often too late to correct the problem with ease. She must expend very large amounts of energy to do so. This frequent delay in understanding eventually leads the loser to assume an attitude of suspiciousness as a general kind of protection, which makes for a rather disagreeable outlook. ("Why are you always lunching with girls, anyway?")

Everybody Is Against Him

The loser begins to see himself as locked in a struggle against the world outside. The battle to overcome his own personal liabilities is never joined, and his chances for growth and improvement are therefore slim. To extricate himself, he has no choice. He must act first to protect himself. If he waits for others to act, he will lose. Thus he acts too soon, too impulsively, on incomplete evidence and is often wrong.

Losers' goals are also too much influenced by what other people think and expect. Thus when the loser reaches his goals even if he believes that luck was not responsible, he may feel that his success is someone else's (the opposing team was lousy, the competing company's salesmen are idiots, etc.).

Since losers have problems managing other people, these others frequently interfere with the losers' plans and disrupt them. Because losers often allow themselves to be pawns without knowing it, they try to set up other people as pawns in retaliation. (Remember what Bucky did to Paul?) Others naturally come to resent being used like this and respond in an angry and punitive way. So there is some basis for the loser's contention that other people get in his way. The truth is that *he invited others to do so*. It is almost as if the loser asks other people to act as policemen to control him.

Because losers are afraid of failing and confronting themselves, they hope to risk as little (and to get away with as much) as possible. So they do too little too late, and almost always end up paying much more and getting much less than they might. And when their belated efforts don't help, they feel cheated and miserable about it.

JUD: Hey, you just bumped into my brand new car!

ED: You're full of crap! Your car was dented before! Look at all those dents! You're just a lousy driver!

JUD: Just a minute! I was parked! *You* hit me!

ED: That's a lie!

WITNESS (*infuriated by Ed's lying*): No, I saw it. You did hit his car.

ED (*to the witness*): What is this? A conspiracy? What're you getting out of this?

WITNESS: I saw it. You hit him.

ED: You're both lying!

JUD: Let's see your registration. I want some facts.

ED: I know my rights! I don't have to show anything.

In a few moments a police officer will be on the scene, and he'll have a lot of unnecessary untangling to do. Jud, who normally would have minimized it all, and the witness, who normally would not have involved himself, are both so angry that they have firmly united against Ed. It was inevitable. And it all started when Ed's first statement denied his fault and projected the feelings he had about himself (that *he* is a lousy driver) onto Jud.

Other losers use less obvious ways to tie a rope around their own necks. They may immediately take on all the blame for anything that goes wrong. They hope to be forgiven. But the loser often does not appear sincere in a stressful situation, and such a confession is usually more than anyone can believe. It is obviously insincere and only makes others angry.

You're Supposed to Love Them, Too

Losers have some interesting ideas in common. Many feel that everyone should love them all the time. Although this may sound perfectly ridiculous, a great many people act as if they expect the world to be like that. Such people are often afraid to express what they really feel; they don't want to risk being rejected. Even though you know who you are and what you want, you can turn out to be a loser when you are afraid to assert those beliefs and demand your rights. Partly, this reluctance is the result of the childhood fear of losing a parent's love by being too aggressive or too selfish.

It is necessary to give in to others from time to time and let them have that last piece of pie. However, to yield all the time will only make you resent your "selflessness" because you know it's phoney. If you don't take what's yours, you will soon feel that the other person is taking your share and you will resent him for it. Or you may expect him to offer it to you. He won't. It would be much better to take your turn.

Losers sometimes lose their turn altogether because they

do not feel worthy enough to take it when it does come around. If you don't take your turn, others will take your place. Since everyone is selfish, you can camouflage this fact with all manner of polite social amenities, but underneath the situation remains the same.

Losers, afraid of giving offense, may postpone taking their turn for a long time. When they finally do, they enrage the very people they were trying not to offend. *Those who took the loser's turn and accepted it as theirs now believe that they are the ones being robbed.* This strong reaction is often enough to convince losers that they were right in not taking their turn to begin with, that they are selfish, and that they should never assert their rights.

Losers see this as proof of their original belief that to demand their rights invites rejection. Nothing is further from the truth. They incite the very rejection they acted to avoid. The fear that losers act upon is self-perpetuating. The person who never takes his turn claims that others prevent him from doing so. Those who try to be loved all the time usually lose and usually bring their losses upon themselves. They end up being hated.

And They Grab All the Credit

Although *privately* losers may not find it easy to attribute victory to their own actions, they *publicly* take all the credit; they feel cheated by the successes of others. Unfortunately, a person who blames others for his failures but takes the credit for his successes invariably creates enemies who will try to put him down and disgrace him.

Successful people are willing to share the credit for their success because they wish to achieve harmony among the people who surround them, whose good will is pleasant and useful to have. Also, they appreciate others' contributions.

The winner remembers that his goal is winning, not taking an ego trip.

If someone gets angry at you for a good reason, not only is this understandable, it may be useful in straightening out difficulties between you. Clearing the air is likely to make any relationship run more efficiently in the long run. It is possible to learn a great deal from another person's irritation with you. The successful person is always interested in having useful feedback from others; losers fear it.

Unlike a loser, a winner is generous with his compliments; rather than being jealous of others, he takes genuine pride in their efforts. He *should* be proud; if those around him function well, it reflects his own ability to manage. When a loser takes all the credit, he demoralizes others and makes them feel unappreciated and unwilling to give their best. As a result, they soon begin to undermine the loser's efforts and help him on his losing way, even if they, too, end up losing in the process.

Resentments that are not immediately expressed in words may eventually make their presence known in other ways. A waiter may spill hot soup on the boss' favorite customer just after the waiter has been put down by the boss; or, tragically, a hunter may accidentally shoot someone he dislikes.

When a loser does lose, all the people whom he had denied credit will chant, "I told you so," just like a Greek chorus. The loser is blamed by everyone for everything that went wrong. *If you want credit for success, you have to accept blame for failure.*

People who are willing to share the credit for success have it much easier if they fail. To begin with, they are less likely to fail—they have others' cooperation. People try harder when they know they will share the credit. With credit goes responsibility; with appreciation, loyalty.

Are You a Leader, a Follower, or a Loner?

Some people are unwilling to work unless they receive all the credit. There is nothing wrong with being the sort of person who does not work well in a team; but then you do best to work alone. If you need all the recognition for yourself, work by yourself and accept your defeats and victories as the result of your efforts.

If possible, leaders should lead, followers follow, loners go it alone.

To place a strong individual worker into a group may make him less efficient, even if the group improves. Indeed, for some people it would be tantamount to making them useless. Unless they are group leaders, creative individuals may not belong in groups, because they do not have the freedom to move flexibly in their customary style. Some successful, creative people are able to see the facts of a situation clearly and wish to act upon them decisively. Others sit on the fence, trying to decide what the issue is, let alone determining what to do about it. They may be unable to explain their actions to the others in the group to the point where they would be able to make the same decision.

Groups can be helpful, but not to the rugged individualist. He will feel slowed down and undermined. His usefulness will decrease. He should avoid groups; his talent for independent thought and action is not best used there. Groups feel threatened by such an individual and are likely to label him a loner, or unconventional. He is; and it is to everyone's advantage in the long run that he is.

A similar situation may develop when a person who functions best in a group is asked to work independently. Good group members often have no great need to stand out. They enjoy sharing ideas with people; the group acceptance and interplay make them feel more complete. By working alone, such a person may feel out of touch with himself, while the responses of other people inspire him.

Not that good group members always depend on reactions of others. They just function best within the framework of a group. It is as if these people see the group as a family. They enjoy contributing to others, helping them reach their best level of performance; they feel fulfilled and are able to contribute. It's all in the family. To work alone might inhibit these same people. (If someone does well in a small group he may do very poorly in a large one because it no longer is a cozy family; it's too impersonal.)

Where do you function best?

Stay there!

The loser always seems to be in the wrong place, trying to do the wrong thing. When he should be on his own, he involves others. When he is in a group, he acts independently.

Although losers do not belong to any specific socio-economic, racial, or religious class, many of them pick up and wave the banners of their race, religion, or economic group. This is their big ploy. Often they disguise the blame for their own personal failure by blaming it on society's oppression of their group.

To get a more accurate picture of such losers, it is only necessary to ask winners from the same group what they think of them. Winners recognize losers immediately. The winners will say that the losers' cause is just, but that his tactics seem to do more harm than good. Losers confuse the issues, bring ill will upon the other members of their group, alienate them, and weaken their cause.

Members of an oppressed group often agree with their leader's goals when he is a loser. They say that his methods aren't always perfect, but at least he is trying to do something. The tragedy is that what he may do about a problem may harm the group. The losers' prophecies are always self-fulfilling.

How To Lose on a Grand Scale

The biggest losers (like Hitler) can appear to be winners at first, offering to correct injustice, to act decisively, or to restore national honor. They are devious and deceitful, deal with half-truths, and play upon the lowest common denominator of feelings in the masses: fear, anger, and greed, the feeling that someone has kept the masses down. They urge the masses into action. When the masses respond positively, the leader takes this as proof that his way is right, and soon he acts more and more on his own without reference to others or even to reality.

No government, no period in history, no political system is without its share of losers: a Hitler, a McCarthy, or a Stalin. Before the world can be a better place, we will have to identify losers who can influence the destiny of fellow men. We must be aware of their particular flaw, whether it is grandiosity, rigidity, or an urgent need to act. It should be possible to identify the action of a prominent national leader as the extension of his own particular flaw and to place that action under review. Men should not die, nor should the precious treasuries of countries be expended in the pursuit of a goal which in reality is nothing more than the distortion of a leader based upon his need for power, for control, for proof that he is manly and strong.

To become winners, people must know how to deal with losers.

Nobody, no matter how bright, how worldly, how successful, or how powerful sees everything exactly the way it really is. Every person has his own style of perceiving the world, a style that depends on the kind of person he is and on his experience.

While nobody sees the truth, everybody has an opinion about it. What you and everyone else brings to a situation—a job, a love affair, or a car collision—is a point of view. Even if another person's ideas seem distorted they may still be enormously useful to you. He may employ other logic and offer another perspsective that might never have occurred to you. In the end you must rely upon yourself to decide, but *your relevance, your impact, and your effectiveness will depend on how well you understand the point of view of others.*

Some people have remarkably clear vision and still lose out because they are able to see events in only one way—their own. They cling to old beliefs and try to judge what happens in the light thereof. Your prejudices make it difficult to perceive new qualities in people and new attitudes in the world around you. You grow rigid if you don't allow for other possibilities.

If you expect to see the same situation every time you look around, or if you feel a need to pigeonhole everything you see in an old category, whether it fits or not, you miss a great deal. The extreme view, and a general attitude of suspicion, is that of the loser. But you can learn to discover a new world by looking through other people's views, just as a lover or a new parent does.

To be successful at this kind of exploration it is useful to be aware of some commonly held attitudes. Even though these attitudes may seem obvious to you, it is surprising how much easier it is to deal with other people if you keep these principles in mind.

People generally fear that their shortcomings are going to be exposed and that such an exposure will make them seem evil or incompetent. At the same time they believe that others are more gifted and able.

People dread being caught for their past errors and being punished. Yet everyone has made his share of errors. Do you remember the last time you were urgently called to see someone important—the boss, the school principal, or the local police chief? Did you wonder which mistakes you were being called down for?

Choosing one goal implies discarding an alternative. Because people generally doubt their ability to make decisions, they fear that they have made the wrong one and suspect that everyone is aware of it and that the bad decision will one day come back to haunt them.

Are You Good at What You're Doing?

People commonly believe that they are unfit for whatever they are doing, although they may not admit it, and may not feel that way all the time. Better watch it: anyone who can make you doubt yourself can control you.

If you wish to manage others, you must first be aware and unashamed of your own limitations and accept them. After all, everyone has limitations. Admitting that to yourself puts you ahead of the crowd. It's like the Hans Christian Andersen fairy tale, "The Emperor's New Clothes." Everyone is afraid to admit that he feels insecure about his worth from time to time.

People fear not only that their faults will be noticed but that they will be pointed out, especially by strangers. One reason why strangers are feared is that they can't be expected to share your point of view and may act unpredictably. The stranger does not know that he is supposed to say that the emperor is dressed. He only knows what he sees: the the emperor is completely undressed.

Since everyone lives in his own head and body and spends considerable time examining his blemishes in the mirror, he is more aware of his imperfections than anyone else is. Indeed, most people are so concerned about themselves that they do not have time to become involved in the details of other people's lives.

In reality *you are not nearly as interesting to other people as you think,* and so your fears of being discovered are usually unfounded. If your weaknesses are revealed to the world, chances are that *you* revealed them yourself without help from others.

Why does this happen if everyone supposedly is trying to keep his shortcomings from being discovered? It's just that the fear of being found out makes people very uncomfortable. Anxiety is hard to live with, which is why children who have done something wrong often get into more trouble just to get caught and be punished in order to feel better again. Let's listen in on a classroom:

TEACHER: Who knows something about the electoral college?

STUDENT (*choking*): Gulp!

TEACHER (*misinterpreting his gulp as a sign of wanting to be called*): Yes?

STUDENT (*paralyzed because his worst fear has been realized*) The electoral college? I . . . oh . . .

TEACHER (*seeing that he doesn't know anything*) Yes? Have you prepared?

From this point on the question is only how much the teacher can get the student to admit. The student's fear of being caught gave him away. The fear of being caught grows until it is worse than the punishment for the offense. People who commit crimes often turn themselves in for this reason. They are suffering and want relief.

Confession in Catholicism and ventilating feelings in psychiatry are both based on the theory that it takes a great deal of effort to keep painful, guilty thoughts to oneself; that letting them out frees a person and allows him to function without needing to get into more trouble just to be punished.

Because other people believe you can see through them and know their faults, give them time and say nothing to correct this mistaken impression and they will begin to confess what they have actually been up to. Remember the man who was selling his house and kept staring at the faulty ceiling? Being a good observer and listener pays great dividends.

Go Ahead: Keep Asking!

Instead of trying to defend your point of view in an argument, try the following technique. Ask the other person what he really is saying. What he really means. What he wants. Why he wants it. What makes it important to him. Ask, but do not attempt to refute his responses. Instead, listen—not only to the words but to *the way he thinks*. Ask yourself some questions, too. How does he reason? Why does he believe he is right?

See if you can determine how his world differs from yours. It does—remember? It has to, just because you are you and he is he. Then try to determine why he sees the world as he does. The replies he has just given you will be your clues. If you arrive at some answers, you may be able to predict his future attitudes and responses.

When you ask others how they feel, or what they think

about certain situations, do so without immediately revealing your own position. Your concerns may have little to do with the other person's and may turn him off. You'll do best to listen first. *Listening without judging or trying to justify your own attitudes is the best way to broaden your view.* It is like climbing a mountain, reaching the top, and seeing the landscape all at once for the first time. (See also Chapter 10).

A warning: you should not pry into matters that are none of your business or try to psychoanalyze or judge others. Stick with the important issue. All you want is to hear the other fellow's side and understand why he feels as he does.

Here's a neighbor trying to clear up a misunderstanding over a pesty dog. One man, Jack, would like the animal tied up because it ruins his yard and terrorizes his kids. Max, the dog's owner, feels that would be cruel. The point is that Jack must respect the owner's feelings for the animal. Only then can he get Max to consider his own. If Jack begins to talk about what a rotten animal Baby is, Max won't even listen to Jack's complaint because his own prejudices will make him place Jack in the category of people who hate his beloved dog.

JACK: Baby (*Baby is a 150-pound Airdale*) sure is a big dog. How long have you had him? (*Meaning: Tell me how you feel about that animal.*)

MAX: Oh yeah. Let's see. I got him when Fluffie died. That'd be almost seven years now. . . .

JACK: Some dog! (*A bland statement encouraging more comment.*)

MAX: Yuh, he sure makes Martha feel safe when I'm away.

JACK (understandingly): He protects her, huh? That must be reassuring to you.

MAX: You bet! I wouldn't feel safe leaving her alone without him. The people around know when there's a stranger in the neighborhood. Baby tells 'em. (*Turns to the dog*) Don't you, boy?

JACK: Yuh. I hear him all the time. You're right, everyone is entitled to protection.

MAX: The way things are today! People get attacked right on the street.

JACK: Yuh. I mean, I'd feel upset worrying that something was going to happen to one of my kids when I was gone. In fact I do worry about that.

MAX: How come?

JACK: Well, this is not very pleasant. I know how important Baby is to you. I mean, you got Baby to replace Fluffie. Well, your dog has knocked my daughter down a couple of times. Once in the street when there was a car coming.

MAX: Oh. Baby wouldn't do something like that! Baby is a tame pup. Would you, boy? . . . Huh? He wouldn't hurt a flea. Good dog!!

JACK: I know you feel that way, but it has happened and more than once. I know that you and I basically see things the same way. You want to protect Martha and I want to protect my kids. I know how much Baby means to you, but I can't replace my kids like you were able to replace your dog Fluffie.

MAX: Well, what do you want me to do? I can't chain the animal up; that would be cruel.

JACK: In some way you'd be right, but you wouldn't want to be cruel to my kids would you?

MAX: Well, no.

JACK: Look, I want to be a good neighbor, just like you do. You think it over and tell me what you want to do about it. I know you don't want my kids to get hurt. Of course you don't! Think about it and we'll talk about it Friday.

Jack sympathized with Max's feelings. He did not put them down. He tried to get Max to see that he felt the same way about his kids as Max did about his dog. It is harder for Max to refute Jack's argument if Jack uses some of Max's own ideas and shows that he understands how Max feels—especially since Jack was careful to point out how much they agree, and not to pressure Max.

The more carefully you ask questions and the more attentively you listen, the more likely it is that you'll find the other person becomes more sympathetic to you. This happens because *people like to talk and rarely have an attentive audience.* (I'll have much more to say about this later.)

In thinking about the other person's responses, you should begin to see some of your own ideas in a new perspective. Even if you don't agree with what he says it is important to listen and determine whose view is most real. This is almost impossible to do by oneself. It takes more than one view to make reality.

Jack has found out something that he hadn't been aware of before. To Max, Baby is really more than just a dog. Baby is a replacement for another beloved pet and is also Martha's protector. Max sees the dog's barking as a note of reassurance, not as a loud annoyance. To complain about the dog without knowing all this beforehand would be like telling Max to leave Martha unprotected. The reality of Max's world is not the same as Jack's. And without understanding that reality, Jack cannot make Max understand the reality of Jack's world; that is, that Baby is a threat to Jack's kids.

Now Jack has built a bridge of understanding to Max and has asked Max to solve the difficulty in view of both realities. This gives Max the opportunity to tell Jack more about how he sees the problem, and it gives Jack an opportunity to present his side of the story again.

Don't Act in the Dark

You need to know how other people feel and to take that into consideration in managing your affairs. To do otherwise is to act in the dark and to invite them to undermine you. Often when you think you are considering the feelings of others, you are really doing no more than considering what you would do if you were in their place. If you act on your assumptions about other's feelings without enough input from them, you may only reveal your own lack of understanding. When you put words in other people's mouths you lose their confidence. They will feel hurt because you do not understand them. In extreme cases they become rebellious because they feel manipulated.

A father who was in the midst of a painful divorce proceeding was confused about how to deal with his children. Understandably he was troubled by feelings of guilt, as are most parents in such situations. Questions came to his mind which he felt must be of vital concern to his children: "Will my children think that I don't love them?" "Will they think I'm hurting their mother and doing it out of anger?" "Will they hate me?" His list could fill many pages of this book.

Severely troubled, he asked a child psychiatrist to help him handle his children (who by this time could sense their father's discomfort and were starting to act uneasy themselves). This only added to the father's problems. The psychiatrist told him to listen to his children and gave him some guidelines to help him see their point of view.

Here is how the conversation with the oldest boy could have turned out without the psychiatrist's help. Note how the father's guilt gets away from him.

FATHER: About your mother and I. . . . First let me say, Jerry, that I do love you very, very much . . .

JERRY (*untying a knot in his yo-yo string*): Yuh. I know. I know.

FATHER: I want you to also know that I know this hurts you and that I don't want to hurt you. (*As if asking to be forgiven*) You do understand?

JERRY (*playing furiously with his yo-yo*): Yuh, I know, I know.

FATHER: You're not mad at me are you?

JERRY (*never looking up*): No, dad.

FATHER: Good, because I'm not mad at you. And you had nothing to do with our problems. I'm sure your mother isn't mad at you either.

JERRY (*yo-yo gets tied up again*): No, she said she wasn't.

FATHER: She did? When did she say that? Put that yo-yo down!

JERRY: Huh? . . . I dunno. She just said it.

FATHER: Well, neither of us is mad at you.

JERRY (*puts the yo-yo in his pocket*): Dad, can I ask a question?

FATHER: Sure, anything, Jerry. . . .

JERRY: Can I have two dollars to go to the movies with Mark?

By playing out his own fears, the father pushes Jerry into a position where he cannot identify with the father's concerns. Father's guilt and sense of weakness only upset Jerry. He just wants to get out of the room.

Actually, Jerry is far from indifferent. He is in a state of turmoil. His house is being torn apart. If Jerry thinks that he caused the divorce it will take much more than one friendly conversation with his guilt-laden father to make him feel better. Most children who become involved in divorces feel upset and do question the strength of the love around them, but usually this is not their main concern. If the child felt loved in the family, the divorce is not going to destroy his self-image. If he does not feel loved, then he only sees the divorce as further proof of his unworthiness.

Jerry has other concerns that trouble him greatly. To find out what is on Jerry's mind, to discover how Jerry sees the world, the father must keep his mouth shut and let Jerry tell him. This is the conversation that did take place after the father listened to the child psychiatrist's advice.

FATHER: Jerry, I know there must be a lot of questions you'd like to ask me. (*Father takes a big breath and holds it, waiting to be asked, "Why are the two of you breaking up?" etc. But he gives no clues to his own thoughts.*)

JERRY (*playing with the yo-yo slowly*): Will I have to move?

FATHER: Huh? Don't be ridiculous! No! Why?

JERRY: Well, Alan's parents got divorced and he had to move.

FATHER: No, you'll stay here. That's silly. This is where you'll be.

JERRY (*winds the yo-yo up, very slowly*): With who?

FATHER: With your mother.

JERRY (*puts the yo-yo down*): Does this mean we're going to be poor?

FATHER: What? No, I'll still be supporting you. You'll have everything you want. Where'd you ever get an idea like that?

JERRY: Alan's father doesn't send them any money.

FATHER: Well, I'll be paying the bills as usual. I'm *not* Alan's father.

JERRY: Will I have to double up in Bobby's room? Alan says that when your parents get divorced you have to double up. (*Spins the yo-yo in a big circle, just missing the light overhead.*)

FATHER: No, everything will be the same. You're not Alan! (*Realizing what he should say in response to Jerry's real concerns*) You'll go to the same school, you'll have the same friends, you'll be able to watch the same television programs. I'll be seeing you every other day. I'll be living twelve blocks away, and you'll come to dinner with me twice a week. . . . And remember, you're still not supposed to twirl that yo-yo inside the house!

This case contains all the essentials of breaking through the barriers to another person's world and reaching him. The father's original view was of little use in helping his son deal with his feelings of disruption and confusion because it was the view from the father's world. Jerry's world was shaped in part by information from his friends. His attitude could not even be guessed at by the father. Jerry's life is his home, his room, his school, and his friends. His parents' feelings bother him, but they are not his feelings. Much of what children feel is expressed without words—for example, Jerry's use of the yoyo.

You must become aware of the enormously varied individual experiences upon which people base their opinions before you can reach them or change their views. To change another person's attitudes usually means to uncover the feelings that lie behind them and then to offer better and more workable alternatives. Coaxing consent by other means is often coercion.

Remember: to the other person *you* are on the other side of the fence and, maybe, standing on the greener grass. Maybe he thinks everything is going your way. He has the same problem that you do. He can only see from his vantage point. Consider what it is he sees and feels, and why. He knows what *his* problems are and probably believes that your problems are minor by comparison. It's part of everybody's childish, self-centered point of view again.

If you want to begin to understand other people you must do so in the same way that Jerry's father reached him: by letting them talk and trying to put yourself in their place.

Always Begin with the Familiar

Concern yourself with the problems that trouble them *right now*. They can't focus on anything else. Begin with something that the other person says bothers him. Try to understand it better. People look for reassuringly familiar objects and familiar faces in a strange setting. His problems are familiar to him. Let him talk about them. You can then move from that point to your own concerns. To begin anywhere else does not allow you to draw similarities; you will have nothing to compare with your problem, nothing will seem similar to him. He will believe he has his problems and you have yours.

Even if the other person understands intellectually what you are talking about, he really won't be interested until he knows that you sympathize with him. To reach other people look for similar feelings and experiences (Jack might try telling Max about a dog he once had that got in trouble.) If you can do this, others will let you enter their world because *they will see you as a kindred spirit*. They will tell you more about themselves just because *you understand*.

Look how Jerry was able to open up to his father once he found out that his father was really interested in what *he* felt. To argue that Jerry should be interested in what his father said, just because his father is his father, is unrealistic. Jerry is interested in Jerry.

Establishing a new common emotional interest often makes it possible to share a new perspective, to look at a situation from a common vantage point. If you wish to be understood and followed, you must first demonstrate that you want to understand the other person. You do not need to understand *everything* at first; very few people do. But showing that you want to understand, being affable, receptive, and accepting will allow others to open up and, in time, to tell you what you do need to understand.

Being open, sharing, and developing a broader point of view makes it easier to get along with others and less likely that they will obstruct you. More likely, they will become friendly if they sense you are sympathetic. Just listening quietly to a problem or saying "It must be very difficult for you" is often enough to make an ally out of someone who would otherwise have been an adversary.

The odd thing about getting through to the other person is that, as you do, that person begins to get through to you, and you are the one who feels he has discovered a kindred spirit. Funny things happen when we lower our barriers.

Three couples who were having difficulty in their marriages were in group therapy. Two of the husbands were professional men. The third was a blue-collar worker. Usually it was the less-educated couple who were able to sympathize with the others in the group and to offer the most helpful suggestions. The others sat back in awe of the laborer and his wife and told them how much insight they had and how bright they were. The self-respect of the working-class couple was bolstered, even though they knew instinctively that their comments were really nothing more than not being hung up with the others' problems. All three couples benefited.

The reason so many problems are so difficult to solve is that people are too close to them. Sometimes the best way to create the needed distance is through the eyes of someone else, someone whose viewpoint is freer of the concerns that blind you.

In this way it is possible to enrich your life and to achieve a greater level of truth about yourself, in feeling as well as in action. Using the reactions of others as barometers to tell you what is going on is more valuable than relying entirely upon yourself.

Watch for "Buzz Words"

Every person responds to "buzz words" that set off short circuits in their emotional make-up. People can pick out a single word on an entire printed page without seeing another word in context—as long as that word pertains to them. Jews pick out the word "Jew," Negroes pick out "Negro," Catholics pick out "Catholic." If you want to use other people's reactions accurately, you must be able to pick out what they consider important. Then you must weigh what they tell you in regard to this bias. You do this now whenever you face a salesman. You hear everything he says as a pitch to purchase.

Everyone's speech is a pitch to purchase his ideas. However, many people do not realize (or won't admit) that they are pitching. They may be unaware of the nature of their own prejudices or unwilling to admit that they are biased. If you understand how and why other people are pitching you, you can draw useful conclusions that otherwise would not be available to you. More than that, you will be less likely to push away a good idea just because it was presented prejudicially.

You don't want to be on the other side of the fence; you just want to stand up high enough to be able to look over and to know what's going on.

8 / HOW TO USE AUTHORITY TO WIN

If YOU KNOW how to handle authority, you're well on the way to becoming a winner. How you handle authority is important because it reflects how well you manage people and how you direct their efforts toward solving a common goal—your goal. Even if you think you have little need to use authority yourself, it can be very helpful to you to understand how authorities use their power, especially when they get in your way.

Any time you assert authority, you assert your leadership, your credibility, and (to some degree) your infallibility. You're saying that you're right and that your ideas are to be followed. You also take a risk. If you are not successful, you may find that you have not only lost the battle, but also the confidence of others in your ability to lead.

When you mishandle authority, other people will know and exaggerate your failure. A leader who makes a mistake may find that his former faithful followers are rebelling against him. No one stirs up the feelings of others quite as strongly as people in authority do.

An authority must understand the source of his power and know how to handle the feelings he evokes in others. An authority is an authority because others believe him to be one; his powers are only those that others believe him to possess.

In some way, all authorities remind people of their parents. Children believe that their parents are strong, right, and all-knowing because children need parents who are strong, right, and all-knowing. Later, as adults, people will project these old feelings of respect, fear, and anger onto an authority and invest in him considerable power *as long as the authority reveals very little about himself* that will detract from their belief.

Children feel angry when their parents tell them what to do, yet often they also feel anxious and guilty about resisting them. Children struggle to control their feelings of resentment toward their parents. Adults feel angry in the same way when an authority tells them what to do; they also try to control their feelings of resentment. An authority's power is derived in part from the fact that others are trying to control these angry feelings which the authority evokes. Some people have poor self-control and find these feelings too uncomfortable to hold inside. So they rebel against authority and undermine the morale of others.

Don't Be Afraid to Assume Authority

Acting with authority to get a job done is not being a phony. It is simply being practical and managing effectively. You do not have to be disliked to act as a leader. You can do so warmly and encouragingly without being a dictator and show genuine appreciation for a job well done.

Look at it this way: if you started to get things done the way you wanted, for a change, don't you think you'd be happier and more willing to praise people, that you'd be easier to get along with? Acting with authority may be your answer, although, like all answers, it won't apply all the time and not toward everyone.

Ten Rules for
Acting With Authority

1. Give short, simple orders and act as if you expect them to be obeyed without question.
2. React immediately and firmly to responses that are not acceptable to you; ask for corrections by issuing a repeat order.
3. Keep your personal life and problems to yourself.
4. Make no inquiries about the personal life of those you lead, except when it has a direct effect on the job at hand.
5. Accept success warmly, but with the attitude that you expected success when you asked for the job to be done in the first place. Attribute success to the fact that your orders were followed.
6. Make requests distinctly and at a slightly slower than normal speed, and wait for a reply.
7. Do not look people in the eye when you speak with them, but look at the middle of their forehead, one-half inch above their eyebrows. This makes it difficult for them to cause you to change your facial expression which is often the first sign that you are backing down. Have a prepared ending ready to cut off conversations. This injects a note of finality and keeps you from appearing awkward.
8. *Do not try to force others to act instantly.* Most people will feel pushed and need a moment to set their thoughts straight. They'll act if you show the authority. Allow for slack.
9. Don't expect to have any friends among those toward whom you act this way; nor should you attempt to cultivate any.
10. When you are wrong, don't admit it as a personal error, i.e., don't say, "I was wrong." Instead say, "The problem would be solved better if —— was done."

If these rules sound rather harsh and impersonal to you, you probably don't know when to use them. They are intended for a situation where one or more people are to be led by a single person. They apply to a teacher and her class, a sergeant and his recruits, a foreman and his men, the boss and his employees, the chairman and his department. They are meant for those who have a task to accomplish and need the cooperation of others.

Following these rules is particularly helpful in a situation where you are the only one aware of an *impending crisis* and must be obeyed to avoid it. It is also useful to act this way when you know you are right and wish to save time in fruitless argument with another person, i.e., a youngster who doesn't want to take proper cold-weather gear when going hiking in the mountains. Finally, when your rights are at stake and you do not wish to debate them, acting authoritatively will help you to assert them.

When Not to Use Authority

It should be obvious from reading these ten rules that they are not suitable for most close human relationships. Something very critical is missing. The authority does not reveal much of his personal life to others; nor does he inquire about the personal life of others.

In relationships between close friends and among family, it is impossible to remain anonymous. Indeed, it would ruin a family if parents acted this way all the time. It is perfectly reasonable to set rules at home, but being generally authoritarian will do considerably more harm than good. Children will resent it, and since a parent is not anonymous, children will look for a parent's faults and point them out to undermine whatever authority exists.

The authority that parents exercise over their children is derived in part from their superior size, strength, and worldliness. A parent's most important influence on his children is not his authority, but his love. If that isn't what it should be, no rules for acting authoritatively will help. They will just make matters worse.

How Much Authority Should You Use, and How Often?

The 10 rules above define a technique for managing people. You may want to use all of them in a difficult situation when you must take charge, or you may use only one technique —such as staring at a salesman's forehead when you don't want to give in to his sales pressure. How much authority you should use varies with the situation and your personality. If you feel uncomfortable acting this way, you should try to practice one rule at a time until you feel familiar with it. *If you don't feel comfortable with these methods, don't use them!* You'll only sound unconvincing, and then you'll be in a worse situation than the one you started with.

In general, *use as little authority as possible to get the job done.* If you use more, people will tend to see you as a bully and will rebel and try to undermine you. Remember: the purpose of using authority is managing others to achieve your goal. If people are already doing what you want, you don't need to show them that you are in charge, that you're the boss, that you have the power. They'll only resent it.

It may sound trite, but it's important enough to emphasize that there's no point in appearing like an authority unless you have something to gain by it. To force people to obey you without question all the time will make you appear ridiculous. *People will not take you seriously, even if they fear you.* And what's worse, when you really need them, they may not respond at all. You'll be like the boy who cried wolf too often.

The Perils of
Being a Chummy Authoritarian

There is a valuable lesson to be learned from the military where even today the officers and the enlisted men are still segregated. This prevents the enlisted men from socializing with the officers and humanizing them; that is, it keeps them from seeing the officers as "regular guys." When a soldier is aware of the human weaknesses of his superiors he is much less likely to follow an order, and it may be an order that will save lives.

Here's another example of what can happen when a leader and his followers get too chummy:

The *Wall Street Journal* described some group leaders in industry who were regarded by their subordinates as aloof, distant, cold, and unbending, but who were nonetheless able to get a great deal out of their employees. These leaders and their workers participated in training groups with the intention of understanding each other's motivations better, hopefully to enhance productivity.

After several meetings, the chiefs did become more aware of their impact upon others. They were more affable, human, and warm. As a result, the Indians felt more comfortable when they were around the chiefs. But—they felt less of a need to work up to the level of their maximum effort because they began to see their chief as just another Indian. The work output of the group dropped. Some leaders even had to be dismissed.

A leader's effectiveness depends on his authority, his willingness to be efficient, to be demanding without regard to others' feelings, and to allow subordinates to project their feelings onto him without trying to correct them. If the workers resent him because he seems like their father, they also obey him for the same reason. If he becomes more human and less of a mystery to the others—as the chiefs did in the group sessions—he loses some of his ability to control them. The Indians can't mistake him for their father anymore; they know him too well.

There is no need for a person who assumes authority to win the prize for being the bastard of the year. You can be kind and show interest in those who work for you, but *you must draw a distinct line between being sympathetic and being chummy*. Being chummy always weakens your authority.

A leader should think of himself as a teacher speaking to his class. He takes charge of others. Their performance pleases or displeases him. He can be warm, friendly, and caring. If he asks for opinions and ideas, it is with the understanding that he will weigh them and determine the best course of action. He may help the others to act democratically and share, but there should be no question about who is in charge. The final responsibility, too, must rest with one person.

Give Others a Purpose

No one's authority can be undermined without his consent. In a time of crisis or confusion, people are very willing to yield their responsibilities to another person. Even if a leader seems wrong, when a situation is desperate people will often follow him merely to have a sense of direction, any direction, just so they can avoid questioning themselves and their values. It's like wanting your parents to come to your aid when the going got rough. (Remember how glad you used to be when they were there to help? You didn't question why, did you?) When times are less confused and people feel more secure about themselves, it is more difficult to assume authority.

Terrifying as it may seem, few people would object to a dictator coming to power and ruling them with an iron hand, if he filled some of the people's basic needs. It's sad to say, but most people are simply too lazy to assert themselves. They are rarely willing to take risks or to give up what they have gained. They fear getting less, and few people value their rights until they lose them.

People do not rise up against dictators when they come

to power—the very time when it would be easiest to overthrow them—because in promising to take care of people, the dictator reminds them of their father. Is it any wonder that politicians kiss babies? The dictator's greatest defense is not the weapons surrounding him but the latent fear of the people that there is something wrong about trying to put down a person who promises material rewards for obeying him—perhaps a better home and more food, just as their father once provided.

Acting with authority is easy in a situation where people already know you and have previously invested authority in you. To control a confused mob is much more difficult. In a mob scene, if someone wields authority as if it were his birthright, others will generally assume that he knows what he is doing. More exactly, they will know that they aren't sure of what *they* are doing themselves. At least they're not sure enough to act decisively, and they'll be pleased not to have to reveal their ignorance by acting. Most people equate acting decisively with knowing what to do. They believe that the person who acts, knows how to act. If he succeeds, they conclude that he knew what he was doing in the first place. If he does not, they're glad it's not their mistake.

Keep Your Doubts to Yourself

The leader must not reveal his doubts or weaknesses to those he wants to lead; it would terrify them and increase their sense of helplessness. I recall watching a fellow medical student take charge of an accident scene. He usurped the authority of the police by announcing that their plans for removing the victim would certainly kill him. In fact, he was not really sure whether the police's methods would have killed the victim. But since he felt that his method would work better, he was not about to debate the possibility with anyone. He gave the reasons he believed supported him, without presenting the opposing arguments. Fortunately, he was right.

Don't Take Resentment Personally

Those who assume authority must be willing to accept *progress* toward their goal instead of *friendship*. People don't like to be reminded that they are too weak to run things, or that they need someone to show them the way. A child struggles to assert his independence, and tries to get away with as much as possible. He may refuse to come home on time at night, and still feel pleased that the parents order him into the house. Then he can say that he wanted to stay out, that he was not afraid of the dark, that it was his parents who made him come in. Secretly he resented his weakness for fearing the dark. And secretly he is pleased to be ordered in. So it is with adults, who resent following orders, and don't like to admit that they are afraid of being on their own. They respect *and* also resent the leader for doing what they cannot.

Act Confident

Political leaders do not need to appear logical—only sure of themselves. They need only state an effect and the contributing causes which they believe are the most important and need give only enough evidence to support these points more or less adequately. If the leader makes others believe that he knows what he is doing, the opposing arguments will seem pale. People will assume that he has considered all the complicated or secret details that are too difficult for them to understand. They're really not! It's just, as I've said, that people are too lazy to think. They believe they must support the leader. The bigger the leader and the bigger the leader's lies, the more likely the mob will believe him. Why? Well, they generally cannot accept (or comprehend) that a leader is lying to them. If an opponent challenges their leader, the masses will generally defend him—not because they believe he is right, but because they are afraid to find that they were wrong to support him and are still afraid of deciding for themselves.

Accept Responsibility

Because the assumption of authority is also the assumption of responsibility, a leader must know *how to deal with failure.* Here's how. Admit that the project in question appears to be in trouble and ask for suggestions for correcting it. Then redirect the efforts of the group to solve the problem. Be careful not to accept all the blame because that would undermine you. If you must point out how others contributed to the failure, do so in private and do it matter-of-factly. Those who are responsible will be grateful. As a way of preserving their image, they may actually support your new position. They do not want to be revealed as failures. If you do reveal their shortcomings publicly, they will try to retaliate in kind. People love to gang up on the person in authority and sometimes they get up enough nerve to do so.

Remember: The Purpose of Being Authoritarian is to Win.

You should not be rigidly attached to any method—only to goals, only to win. No leader can be familiar with all methods, nor should he pretend to be. The leader's job is to set goals and make certain they are met. His expertise is in knowing how to lead, how to win, not in knowing all the details that need to be attended to along the way. It would be his undoing to try to do so. Details are the business of subordinates.

One of the most effective leaders I know is a businessman with four years of liberal-arts education, who took over a large technical industrial complex when it was very much troubled by inefficiency. The former directors had doctorates in the sciences and worked closely with their employees in solving problems, but their company was going bankrupt. The first day he took over, the businessman walked around the factory and stopped to observe one of the company's products, a machine that required two men to operate and produced one hundred rolls of wire each hour. He called a meeting and gave his first instructions: "Make a machine that requires only one man to run it and puts out two hundred rolls of wire an hour." Everyone said it was impossible. He said only, "Show me the plans in one week." The company developed the machine, and in a year had improved its financial situation immeasurably.

The methods I have discussed in this chapter may not be the ways one should function in the best of all possible worlds, but this is not the best of all possible worlds. Whether people aspire to follow a leader because his cause is noble or because he is in league with the devil, they have the same reasons for staying in line. They may fear disapproval. Or wish to control bad feelings. Or they may want to avoid responsibility for their actions, preferring the anonymity of the group. Or they may fear being exposed. It's a fact: *man is led to noble acts more out of fear than out of inspiration.*

Our society is founded in part upon a concept of fear. We have built a military system on the need to have a strong deterrent against an enemy. Our law is based on the fear of punishment. Even if that were not the original intent, that is how it functions.

In a society whose institutions function by the use of fear, fear becomes the way authority is exercised. By the same token, fear is the way in which authority is undermined.

No matter how noble your cause, how just your God, how benevolent your intentions toward your fellow man, your success could depend on how well you use authority to implement your plans—and, in doing so, how you make use of the fear in others.

What if an Authority Gets in Your Way?

Now that you know how authorities function, it is useful to consider what to do when an authority begins to encroach on your rights. Do not try to undermine a person's authority by acting in ways that run counter to his rules. That is: do not try to make him act chummy with you; do not make him reveal his doubts; do not try to involve him personally. Any authoritarian worth his stuff is immune to a maneuver like this. He will see your attempt to be friendly (or undercutting) as a sign of your insecurity, an indication that he should continue being rigid, and he will ignore your protests.

Handle him by acting like an authority yourself in asserting your rights. It is simply a matter of protecting your territory. Remember the points mentioned in earlier chapters. Make sure you want to fight the battle. Go at it with everything you have, once you have made the decision. Be certain you believe in what you are doing. You will be surprised how quickly authoritarian people back down once they know that you intend to fight for your rights. They are not prepared for that. To risk losing an unnecessary fight and weaken their base of power is the last thing they want.

Do not hesitate to go over the head of any authority once you see he is inflexible and unreasonable. Appeal to the highest authority who will listen, and do so in a reasonable, logical, unemotional way, stating your case clearly. Indicate to the higher authority that you find it difficult to understand the rigidity of your adversary. If you've done your job well, the higher authority will feel he must act to set the situation straight.

IT'S WORTH SAYING AGAIN, and emphatically: Knowing how to listen to others and how to get them to open up and talk is the single most important skill you need to win.

You cannot possibly know *everything* you need to make a success out of your life, and it is most unlikely that you could ever gather even just the readily available information all by yourself. It follows that you must depend on others for much of your data. Being able to get another person to share *his* knowledge and experience in a free and cooperative way is invaluable. You gain nothing less than the benefit of another's entire life experience.

Little of what happens in one's daily life is really important; most is repetitive routine. Since only a handful of events proves memorable to each person over the years, it is possible to share the most valuable experiences of others in a fairly short time. But to do this intelligence-gathering efficiently you must know how to direct your conversations with your sources to elicit their candid opinions about the subjects that concern you.

Since one of most people's greatest fears is that they will be found lacking and will therefore be rejected, the first step in getting someone to open up is to counter this fear. This works best by giving some reassuring indications that this won't happen with you. Here's how to drop such hints:

Be accepting and willing to take in whatever is said without being judgmental;

Listen carefully and ask the kind of question that seems to be generated by listening to a *fascinating and bright person*;

Don't sound probing;

Convey that your interest is generated by a mutual concern, by an understanding of the other person, or by his charm.

The larger point is that you must be genuinely interested in the other person, and without malice. If you are out to be devious and to use what you learn to the disadvantage of others, you will give yourself away and your efforts will boomerang. These techniques all depend on developing *a sense of trust*. The slightest insincerity will do you in. And if it does, I'm sure you deserve it.

Listen to a young man trying to make the acquaintance of a woman at a party.

HE (*appears fascinated*): I'm sorry, but I overheard you talking about Denmark.

SHE (*enthusiastic*): Yes, I just got back!

HE: What impressions did you have of the place?

By asking for her impressions, he is putting her ever so slightly on the spot. She has to reveal something of herself.

SHE: Oh, very quaint. Especially Copenhagen. I loved it.

HE (*picking up her enthusiasm*): Sounds charming. Sounds like you had fun.

He uses the word "charming," meaning quaint, just to agree with her feelings at an early stage in the conversation so that she feels he approves of her. He tries to agree with her *feelings* more than with specific ideas.

SHE: Oh, it was! They have all these lovely lakes with swans and boats on them, and tiny villages.

HE (*still follows her enthusiasm*): That sounds great. It must be beautiful.

He agrees but still stays non-specific. He only asks open-ended questions and avoids asking questions like, "How many lakes were there?" because that might be answered with one word that could end the conversation. The conversation had best consist of him asking for her impressions and approving of them, and of her sharing her feelings with him. This kind of conversation becomes addicting to her because she enjoys being approved of. Everyone does. Soon, other ideas go on display; at first they are related to the original topic but then they just flow. It's just a matter of the man's allowing it to happen and accepting the young lady's feelings and enthusiasm.

She will feel that she is revealing much of herself. By not judging what she says, he allows her to feel, "He is just like me." He establishes a common ground, based on approval of her acts and feelings. People tend to value people who approve of them.

The Other Person Can't Help but Reveal Himself

As you try this, you will get a pretty good indication of the other person's attitude toward life—what the major issues in the other person's life are—just by listening and letting the other person tell you what is important to him. After a while the young man will know that his new tourist friend is interested in child-care programs, just like those in Denmark; that she feels most people are too aloof; that material values are unimportant to her.

You do *not* need to make great insightful comments to appear insightful. All you need to do is to listen and to try to understand the other person. Ask how and why they think and feel the way they do. So very few people ever do this that your approach will appear refreshing and you will be regarded as kind and intelligent. People make the assumption that *good* listeners are exercising good judgment to be listening to them.

It is also important to know how to use silence when dealing with people. Psychotherapists often use a nondirective technique of interviewing people. They let their patients do the talking, being largely unresponsive to them in order to draw them out further. An alternative method is to repeat the last few words or phrase of a person's sentence so as to urge him to talk further:

> PATIENT: I went out today.
> THERAPIST: You went out today?

This usually works very well, but should the other person discover what you're doing he may clam up and feel intruded upon. Using silence is tricky. It creates a great deal of anxiety in the other person because it forces him to decide how and whether the conversation should go. If you try to influence someone by using only silence you may fail simply because the person will avoid you to avoid the anxiety you create. Improperly used in psychotherapy, silence creates needless anxiety and often drives patients away from issues that need to be explored.

Silence can also hide the therapist's ignorance. A simple redirecting question or statement based on revealed feelings is often preferable and more effective.

> PATIENT: My boss doesn't understand how difficult my job is. He just makes demands, just like my wife.
> THERAPIST: Sounds like you feel taken for granted.

Another tactic which helps keep the other person talking is to react to his comments with an accepting yet noncommittal positive comment, such as "Really," "Tell me more," "No kidding," "I bet that was fascinating," "Great," or, "That's ter-rific."

People seldom hear these comments in conversations and so they very much appreciate this kind of approval. Even though they may suspect that the comments are mechanical, people will still reach out (and talk) to earn more of them. Merely nodding your head in agreement and smiling is a sur-prisingly rewarding version of the same technique for encour-agement.

Keep the Other Fellow Talking

Instead of responding to specific details when you make your comments, stay alert and see how well the other person is opening up and how the flow of words is progressing. Then respond to that. This will make your comments sound more genuine, and they will be.

Instead of making the other person fall silent (as a spe-cific probing question might do) your comment will be an in-centive for the other person to keep talking. The other person will respond positively when you comment, "Go on," "That's very good," "I like that," "Good," "Yes," "Sure," "Certainly," "Of course," or, "Now you're talking." He will be talking, and he'll be enjoying it. Since everyone appreciates a good listener, you'll be developing a good reputation besides.

You can choose to agree with the other person at almost any time, but disagreeing—unless it is carefully qualified—can end the conversation. Try: "I think you're mistaken, but per-haps I don't understand." Do avoid words that are negative: "Wrong" or "No", etc.

To expand a conversation, ask additional questions, such as, "What do you mean?" "Can you explain that?" "I don't understand," "How does that follow?" "What does that mean?" "Why do you say that?" or "Why are you asking that?" These questions will enable you to manage almost any conversation and keep it moving. An extremely important question to ask is, "How do you feel about that?" But keep in mind: once you ask it you are committed to listen and to allow a wide range of subjects to develop. *To be a good listener you must be genuinely interested in discovering what the other person has to say.*

The style I've just described places one person essentially in the role of directing rather than participating. Little is said that reveals much about the opinions or attitudes of the director. The primary objective of this technique is to learn as much as possible from (and about) the other person. It is a tool for interviewing, not a style adaptable (or appropriate) to most casual conversations.

Little about oneself is brought into the conversation in the early phases because it would only detract. Imagine how slowly events would move if the other person were to become involved with the way you feel and think—and if he tried to win your approval—when you need to know some specific facts from him to form an opinion about a business matter. Imagine how difficult it would be if the personnel manager told a new job applicant all about his new baby. He wouldn't know enough at the end of the hour to form an opinion except that the applicant said that the baby was cute, which he would be a fool not to say.

The Art of Becoming a Kindred Spirit

If you wish to have a person side with you, it is important that you understand the goals and ideals toward which he had been striving all along. Once you are more certain of those goals, and the kind of person you're dealing with, it is possible to introduce some of your own viewpoints. You should do so with great care, first introducing those which the other person is most likely to agree with. In this way you present yourself best: first as a good, sensitive, and warm listener; then, as you include your own viewpoint, as a kindred spirit. After that it is possible to bring up your less familiar or less popular ideas because you've first established the strongest possible mutual agreements.

As soon as other people discover that they are *safe* with you, and that you genuinely approve of them, they will begin to open up even more. Everybody needs to share his feelings, but most people fear that when they open up they will be rejected or will be branded as miserable, cruel, and selfish. If you believe that you, too, are selfish and that there are very few acts which other people commit that, given the same circumstances, you could not be capable of, you can learn to be *accepting*. Certainly, all people have the same basic feelings: love, hate, fear, etc.; and even the most socially offensive crimes have fleetingly crossed most people's minds. To accept that is to accept the way man is.

Given an accepting person to talk to, people will usually reveal themselves, seeking to confess their sins and to find acceptance in their listener's eyes—if you give them enough time and do not indicate that you will use what they tell you against them or to hurt them. Most people who would hurt others already have a reputation for treachery; it precedes them and turns other people off early in a conversation. If you intend to use the information that others reveal to you so you'll get along better with them—through understanding—the relationship will grow.

Since the success of this technique depends on your sincerity and the ability to develop trust, it will almost always fail in the hands of those who intend to misuse it. This technique should not be used to force people to do anything they do not want to do, but rather to help understand how to manage them so that they live and work better and so that their problems are more easily handled. It also allows you to help people achieve their maximum productivity.

It's Useful to Remain a Stranger

People sometimes reveal their weak spots when they are in a conversation with a perfect stranger, confessing shortcomings that they would never tell anyone else (a hitchhiker may tell his life story to the driver). This atmosphere of remaining a stranger can be cultivated in a conversation by remaining anonymous. Its limitations are in the nature of the relationship. You can't be anonymous to a friend.

When you are aware of another's weak spots, it becomes possible for you to take them into consideration and to act in ways that allow him to function more effectively, rather than making him struggle. If you know a man badly needs to be esteemed, don't assign him to the complaint department where he'll be berated all day.

A person's weak spots can be used to win him over to your way of thinking. This is not as diabolical as it may sound on the surface. You are not using other people's secrets to twist their arms and *force* them to accept your ways. Nothing could be more dangerous. After telling you about themselves, other people will generally have a certain expectation that you will treat their information with confidentiality and will not hurt them with it. They will have the feeling that they trusted you, which they did, and if you break a trust like that you can expect their wrath to descend upon you like nothing else you have seen before.

There are other risks in letting someone open up to you. Because people are frequently unable to accept the responsibility for their own shortcomings, they will seek out someone to blame. If someone told you all of his faults, it is very tempting for him to see you as the cause of some future trouble. Who knows—if you misused their information they could be right, especially if you sent that poor fellow to work in the complaint department, knowing (because he told you) how much pain he feels when he is rejected.

How To Win Easily Without Using Power

If you use power to change others' minds, getting other people to come over to your way of thinking is impossible to do. People aren't built like that. Every point has two sides, and most people have a tentative belief in both and vacillate between the two possibilities. To win an argument you should agree with those of the other person's beliefs that are closest to yours.

This has the advantage of developing a sense of mutuality. People will gradually reveal opinions about issues you are interested in. You should agree *very strongly* when the other person's ideas fit in with your own. In so doing you make him feel rewarded for agreeing with you and less ambivalent about your views. You motivate him to agree with you even more. Remember: there are two sides to each feeling, and the reason people choose one side over another is that they fear the other choice. By agreeing with them when they state points in support of your side, and by accepting them, you help them to associate good feelings with your views. They learn to associate your side with pleasure.

The best way to convince another person to adopt your idea is to give him credit for having thought of it. This is the most effective, most rapid, sure-fire way of winning at almost anything. In order to succeed at this method, follow these simple steps.

1. Begin the conversation in a general nonthreatening way; present the problems as if asking advice.
2. Ask the other person for his suggestions and opinions.
3. Pronounce the advice *"brilliant"* as soon as any fragment of your idea appears.
4. Restate the fragment with "You mean . . .", filling it out more completely with your idea.
5. Praise the other person for the idea and allow him to elaborate on it.
6. Tell someone else about "his idea" in front of him and get that person to agree with your opinion of it.

This is much easier to do than you might expect. People are very vain; they *need* to be thought of as brilliant. To demonstrate how strongly a person's ideas can be reinforced with approving attitudes and how this alters the content of their speech, the following experiment was tried some years ago.

During an interview, the number of responses in which a subject referred to color were counted. During the second interview with the same subject the interviewer responded positively to any color response by smiling, nodding, or looking pleased. These responses were counted. During the third interview the interviewer responded normally again. During the third hour the number of color responses counted as twice as high as the first hour, as the subject tried to elicit approving responses.

Go Ahead: Give the Other Person the Credit

Allow people to work for your approval by accepting your ideas when they mention them. When you have been able to implant your idea in them and given them the credit and approval for thinking of it, they will embrace your idea more firmly than ever. This works whether the person or persons involved are children, spouses, people who work for you, policeman—anyone. Remember: losers feel they *own* part of winners' ideas when they are successful. Anyway, attributing your idea is a good way of getting cooperation:

BOSS: There seems to be trouble with accounts again! Falling behind.

CLERK: Yuh. I know. It's a mess. It's that damn bookkeeping system in the electronic division. You can't make heads or tails out of it.

BOSS: It's bad, huh? Can't figure it out? Maybe it needs to be changed, updated, so we can tell how old accounts are.

The boss mostly restates what the clerk said, so that the source of information will keep on talking. Notice especially that the boss does not chastise. He's just trying to get the facts:

CLERK: We should do something like that.
BOSS: I agree.
CLERK: They need a new system!
BOSS: That's a good idea!
CLERK: It sure is! They need a system where the accounts are separated by length of time overdue, the action needed to collect them, and have notices sent to the salesmen so they stop selling to those accounts.
BOSS: That's tremendous! That's one of the best ideas I've ever heard. Why don't you draft out a page showing how to do it? I'll do what's necessary to make sure the department gets reorganized your way.

Most problems and most arguments will seem much more difficult (and less clear cut) than this to resolve. The main point is: begin to use this tool of offering your ideas for others to adopt as theirs and apply it as often as possible. As you get used to handling ideas in this way, it will become easier for you to succeed because you'll have the *help* of your potential opponent. You will discover that life will move along much easier for you, and for others as well.

The key to understanding people, then, is to listen; to know what to listen for; and to know what to accentuate and what to encourage. To discourage and *disagree* rarely does anything but make another person raise his guard, become suspicious of your intentions—and look for reasons to disagree with you in turn. If a person does not feel the need to overcome you or to win over you, and you do not appear to be trying to do the same, you are managing properly.

Some people can be best handled by making a clear, forceful statement instead of going through all of this time-consuming effort. Mostly they are children or people who are so dependent that attempts to listen to them reveal little about them that is helpful. Dependent people very often *try so hard to agree with what you say* that these methods may not work. The dependent people play the listening, reacting game all their lives. However, they will scream when events do not go their way.

If the first rule is to listen, the second rule is not to *blame* anyone for a problem. Merely state the problem as you see it. Finally, *attribute* your solution to someone else, hopefully someone who is going to be able to clear that problem up.

People are most proud of ideas that are their own, and they love (and are loyal to) people they believe are appreciative of them.

EVEN WHEN you do everything right, if you do not create the right *impression*, winning cannot be guaranteed.

Even before they hear you speak for the first time, others are already scrutinizing your presence and are forming an opinion about you. The impression that you create comes from what others *think* they see or hear, as well as what they *actually* see or hear. For instance, if you resemble someone familiar to another person, someone who is associated with bad feelings—perhaps a boss who once fired that person—you are already on the way to forming a bad impression.

You can usually tell when something like this is going on because it's happening so early in the encounter. Believe in yourself. Assume that the cold reaction you're getting from the other side is not of your doing. Try not to react to it. Try to appear pleasant. If you get irritated, this will only strengthen the other person's belief that you are like the unpleasant person you remind him of. Being pleasant gives you a fighting chance.

When you first meet others *you* are the stranger; as such, you represent the unknown to them and are *feared* until they can relate you to people or goals that are familiar to them. Not to be able to place someone in a familiar category seems to create uncomfortable tension. Categorizing people relieves some of the uncertainty. You may be associated with a very unsavory character in the minds of the people you wish to impress merely because you both have the same hair style. The opposite could also happen.

There is no short cut to discover how you appear to others. You could ask people what they think of you directly, but that would not be very accurate; few people like that sort of question and few would answer honestly. It is better to observe how others act toward you and to guess what they are responding to.

Because the right kind of impression determines the attitude that you'll have to live with or try to overcome it is impossible to overestimate the importance of creating one. If your attitude evokes feelings of anger in others, they may be deaf to your ideas and will be suspicious and not give you the benefit of the doubt. This is a serious problem to overcome. At best it will slow you down in getting what you want; at worst it will destroy your chances altogether.

Opposites Do Attract

Fortunately there is a way to give the right impression. Figure out what kind of person you are dealing with, and act accordingly.

Some personalities get along very well with some people and badly with others. For instance, dependent people are often attracted to those who are independent and strong-willed. Controlling people are often attracted to people who are vivacious and open, who possess the spontaneity that the controlling types lack. Competitive people may be attracted to an authoritarian —only to try to put him down later.

It is difficult to assume an attitude that is not characteristic of your own style of personality and carry it off convincingly. Very few people are really first-rate actors, especially when the stakes are personal. Besides, *the point of this chapter is not to teach you how to masquerade but how to avoid offend-*

ing so that you will get *a fair chance*. Indeed, if you try to be another personality, it is an open invitation to disaster. Nothing puts a person off more than seeing someone artificially trying to be the kind of person he likes best. The result of such an attempt will invariably be that you will be compared to other people he already knows, and prefers; you'll be found lacking and solidly rejected as a phony. If you try to show a dependent person that you *are* an authority while you're actually not, he'll know it because he's spent his life reacting to "real" authorities. This does not mean that you can't act with a sense of authority as long as you're being yourself. You can, and if you do it well you'll be respected by a dependent type. But don't try to fool him.

First: Be Bland!

Assuming that you know what is expected of you, how do you give the right impression? The answer is not difficult to understand, and if you keep in mind the previous chapter on how to listen, it should be fairly easy. When you desire to create a specific impression *you should at first not try to give an impression at all*.

At the beginning, the only active role you should take is to prevent creating an impression opposite to the one you desire. Remember: you are the stranger, and that's a deficit.

Listen! Listen to make sure you know what the other person wants. Does he wish to impress you? Or to be liked? Or to be respected?

By agreeing with specific points he makes, you can create the desired impression; you can emphasize how impressed you are, how much you like or respect him. After a while he will make you aware of other attitudes and ideas that are part of what he finds desirable in another person.

The best first step is to *find out what he considers to be the worst impression and to avoid making it*.

Watch this young man meeting a prospective father-in-law. The fiancee's family is very wealthy. The older man is suspicious of the young men who court his daughter. He often breaks relationships apart. Our young man is in love with the girl. Her family money is not unattractive, but he is primarily interested in the girl. He wishes to convey the appearance of sincerity. The girl's father is very provocative, very angry. The pitfall is to appear money-hungry.

FATHER: Susan said you'd be by. What's this all about?
HANK: Susan and I are very much in love and are talking about marriage.

Note that he says "talking about," not "are going to get married." It's less threatening.

FATHER: What are you planning to live on, your good looks? You'd starve in that case. What do you suppose she sees in you?

It's best to answer taunting or stupid questions in a way that cuts them off politely—or not to answer them at all. Don't pick up on them! They're just ways of diverting you from a painful subject.

HANK: I have plans.
FATHER: I bet you have! Well, I'm not going to support you.

Try to show a reaction that indicates the same attitude as the threatened person. It takes the pressure off, lowers his guard.

HANK (acting almost put out): I certainly hope not!
FATHER: What's that?
HANK: I think the fastest way of undermining any mari-

tal relationship is to take away the husband's authority. What would the wife have to respect?

FATHER: Yes!!! Yes???

Pause as long as necessary here. The old man is on the defensive. He has to form a new attack. Don't worry, he'll come up with something.

FATHER: Well, where are you planning to live?
HANK: That depends . . .

The father has just asked the same question as before, i.e., "What are you planning to live on, my money?" If you don't yet have an answer, tell your plans only insofar as you have them. Remember: *no one knows all the answers!* Indeed, only a fool thinks that he has everything all figured out. The way in which you go about figuring situations out impresses people more than your answers. Confidence is built upon the belief that *you can manage*:

FATHER (*continuing*): *Depends on what?*
HANK: I'll be finishing graduate school and have applied for a grant. I have a job in the department, teaching. This entitles me to university housing. And a firm in the area will take me part-time. Susan says she's interested in working, too. So we'll do quite well.

FATHER: Susan working? Why, she never had a job in her life!

HANK: I suppose there was a time, sir, when someone could have said that about you, too. You can't judge a person before you've seen them perform. Susan will do fine!

Hank pleads his case intelligently when he asks Susan's father not to judge her too soon, and he shows he has opinions, too; but note: *he gets brave defending Susan, not himself*:

FATHER: Well, what do you expect from me?
HANK: Your blessing.
FATHER: That's all?
HANK: That's a great deal!

Now he's done it! He has shown respect and turned the tables, all at the same time.

In general, you give the proper impression by being aware beforehand of what that impression consists of, and also knowing what will ruin it. Most people who have trouble making the right impression either don't know what is expected of them or don't think the situation is serious enough to warrant their full attention. They are too casual about it. Rarely does someone not know how to act in a situation *once he knows what is expected of him*. This usually takes only a moment to figure out, but it's easy to be lazy, and easier still to sit back and try to play it by ear. *Don't ever leave impressions to luck.*

To determine what attitude is expected, consider:

1. What kind of person the other man is, i.e., dependent, controlling, competitive;
2. What the other person's goals are (being loved, keeping control, winning esteem);
3. What he is afraid of (losing someone, losing control, losing face).

Construct a plan that is responsibe to *his* goal and take *his* fears into consideration by avoiding discussion of them at first.

For example, Hank would rate Susan's father as (1) controlling, (2) interested in keeping control, and (3) afraid of losing control. Therefore, he does not announce the engagement as an accomplished fact because this would only throw the father into a rage, and force the old boy to try to exert some control by breaking up the lovers just to prove to himself that he still is in power.

The way to create the best and most lasting impression —let me say it again—is to find people who are interested in the *same* ideas and the *same* goals and who wish to use the *same* methods to reach them as you. Unfortunately, the odds on finding such people are slightly better than finding the Abominable Snowman at a formal reception for the Queen. People are different—and we therefore find them difficult.

To reach a difficult person, do not offend him. This means that you should try to get him to expound on his attitudes, opinions, and comments as they relate to the particular subject at hand. You need not agree with him. Indeed, if you cannot, you must not try to pretend that you do. Hank could have asked his future father-in-law to tell him how *he* started out, what obstacles *he* faced and how *he* overcame them. Just listening patiently to another's argument creates the feeling that you are sympathetic to it. Remember that such people are suspicious of you anyway and are quick to pick up your lack of sincerity, after which you won't stand a chance of convincing them of anything.

Although you should not try to agree if you can't do so convincingly, do not disagree with them. Instead, indicate that you are not sure yet and need to know more. They'll gladly tell you more. Do not try to impress the other person; merely encourage him to continue talking and to reveal how he feels. The more he says, the clearer your understanding will be. It may be possible after a time to try to alter his approach by agreeing with those of his ideas that approach yours and by using some of the techniques explained in the chapter on listening.

In general, people see others the way they want to see them. If you need a villain, you'll find one. People broadly group others into one of two categories: they're *"like me"* or *"not like me."* To rule, control, win arguments with, manage, direct, teach, or in any other way influence people, first try to understand what qualities are needed to fit into their "like me" category. Hank's prospective father-in-law considers the qualities of hard work, self-sufficiency, honesty, integrity to be "like me." Hank's statements tried to give the same impression, and he became a winner.

It is only after you are aware of what the "like me" label means to another person that you can hope to reach him. To create a winning impression is to make the other fellow believe that you both have a great deal in common.

Before you develop your own private system for winning, you must determine exactly what it is you want. You may respond by saying that you already know what you want; but you probably don't. Most people don't. They probably wouldn't recognize what they claim they want if they had it in their hand.

A person's *desires* are generally much greater than his *needs*, and even when needs are momentarily satisfied, desires characteristically grow. It seems that the more a person has, the more he thinks he needs to be happy. Greed is a very peculiar drive; it seems to feed upon itself. Look at the simple demands that you made years ago. How pale they seem next to your present plans!

Desires grow more in response to feelings than to reality. When people feel empty and hopeless about themselves they often try to solve this personal discontent by gobbling up more possessions. Or they scramble to fulfill another person's goals in the hope that they'll at least win praise and acceptance. But this kind of "success" cannot satisfy them because it is not theirs.

Others do not accept the present for what it offers. They compare it to the future, which always seems so much better. They are consequently unable to enjoy what they have, even though it is more than they hoped for years ago.

There are many ways to discover your goals. And once

you do, you must evaluate them to see whether they are realistic or not, or whether they are just another escalation of desires that may not be worth a struggle to fulfill.

How To Make a List of Goals

A good way to begin to find out what your real goals are is to make a series of lists comparing your goals at different times in your life. The idea is to see whether they changed and then to try to understand how and why they did.

Begin by making a list of the goals you had at age fifteen, putting down as many wishes you had for yourself as you can remember in the order you think of them. Make another list of the goals you had at age twenty or twenty-five. Then make lists for your goals at age thirty, forty, fifty, and so on. It is useful to have the ages of the first lists closer together because more change and growth occur in one's early years.

One of the first things you should notice is that many of your early *materialistic goals have long been fulfilled.*

You will get as much out of these lists as you put into them. The more honest you are, the more helpful you will find this self-evaluation. You can sometimes determine at a glance whether or not your goals and desires are running you ragged because they have been expanding beyond any reasonable chance for you to control them.

The following lists were prepared by a fifty-year-old advertising executive who constantly complains that he has little time to do what he really wants and that he never has enough money. His lists are fairly short, indicating how reluctant he is to look at himself. They are very much colored by his personality, expressing a need to control.

GOALS AT 15
To be an artist, living abroad
To leave home

To get some experience with girls
To have enough money to do what I want

GOALS AT 20

To give a one-man show
To study painting in Paris
To make a million
To have a job using my talent

GOALS AT 25

To continue painting
To settle down and get married
To have more money
To have more control over my advertising ideas

GOALS AT 35

To have enough money for college for the kids
To have a stronger voice in agency policy-making
To have my own agency some day
To paint for a year without worrying about anything else

GOALS AT 45

To have more control over clients' attitudes
To be able to take life easier and still have agency function
To have more security
To have more free time for hobbies

Apparently the wish for money is ever-present with this man. Not only does it reflect his desire to be secure, but it has displaced his wish to paint. As a younger man he wanted to be an artist, but he was afraid he'd fail, and so he substituted external security for internal fulfillment. His need for self-expression is not filled by making money, but he doesn't know that.

Owning an agency is not the same to him as being an artist. So he substituted having more control over the agency for becoming a painter. At twenty-five he wished to have a voice in the account; at thirty-five he wished to have control over the agency; and then at forty-five he wanted control over the client.

Because he is not satisfying his inner need to paint, the more he wants to control outside himself.

The security that he desires centers superficially on having more money, but judging from his lists it does not seem as if he'll *ever* have enough. One would guess that he is very controlling of the people in his agency and that his influence probably stifles them. If he wishes to have control over everything, he must manage most of the accounts and be personally responsible for them. Because he is unwilling to delegate power to others or allow any part of the company to get out of his grasp, the number of accounts his agency is able to handle is limited. The fact that his goals do not vary much also reflects his rigidity.

Because his control restricts the company's growth, his financial needs are not met. If he were able to satisfy them, he could paint again. He must decide whether to decrease his control over the accounts and increase his company's productivity, or accept the idea of having all the control but not enough money.

People who are enmeshed in this sort of conflict always try to have it both ways. They must determine whether or not they can *ever* feel comfortable managing the way they currently do. If they cannot, they should change. This man should see that by relinquishing control in the agency now he would have more control, i.e., security, in the years ahead. This should help him to *yield control in the present in exchange for security in the future*—plus give him the freedom to paint.

When Are Materialistic Goals Real?

It is difficult to tell when materialistic goals are real and when they mask a wish such as wanting to be an artist. Material goals (i.e., a need for an ever-larger home) often disguise goals that are not worked at because the fear of failure is too great. The only one who can determine what goal is "for real" is you, and the best time to do it is when you make your list.

Your lists will probably be more extensive than the adman's. Besides material goals, you should include such attitudes as peace of mind and other personal wishes. Also, compare these feelings to see whether they have changed, and how, and try to understand why. You will get a clearer idea of those goals which you have not been able to attain or perhaps have even been unaware of. A pattern may appear from list to list and help you to discover a trend you never saw before. If you do, you will be more aware of what you really want from life and from those around you. Because you will find it much easier to pinpoint your needs, you will be more willing and better able to give up unimportant desires and concentrate on those goals that can really contribute the most to make you happy.

When you think about goals, ask yourself whether your goals are really *your* very own. Have you perhaps adopted the ideals of another person merely to try to please him? The fact that you adopted someone else's goal is often forgotten long after the goal has become an established part of your routine. This alone can make life seem pretty unrewarding. Next, it is important to take a good look at your achievements and compare them carefully both to the goals you now seek to reach and to your former goals as well.

A Housewife's Sample Lists

The following lists were made by a thirty-four-year-old housewife with two children. This woman comes from a very closely knit family. She is very attached to her parents, especially her mother, who believed that a woman's place is in the home or doing socially acceptable committee work.

GOALS AT 15
To be most popular in school
To achieve something that would make my family proud
To be respected by my friends

To have a large family and a big home
To have a career

GOALS AT 20

To be president of my sorority
To be a student speaker at graduation
To have my own apartment after graduation
To become a social worker
To make my parents proud of me

GOALS AT 25

To be president of the PTA, The League of Women Voters,
    and the Woman's League!!
To be a member of the school committee
To have a bigger house
To spend more time traveling
To have a summer place
To have a real fur coat
To show my mother that I'm as good as she is
To keep my husband happy
To have more time to spend reading
To be a good mother
To do charity work
To have more money
To be happy

GOALS AT 30

To have more time
To feel I have accomplished something
To keep my family the size it is
To work with people

This woman's lists are very interesting. They reflect the struggle between pleasing her mother and pleasing herself. Even now she does not seem to have found herself. Notice how her wish to become a social worker ended abruptly. It was at this time that she decided under pressure to give up the idea of a career and get married. Mother frequently expressed the notion that a wife could not have a career. Afraid of displeasing mother, she decided at twenty-two to become as socially useful as possible within the guidelines of what would be acceptable to mother; that is, to be active as a club woman.

Over the years she became increasingly concerned with being respected. She implimented this goal by becoming president of many organizations. But it is obvious from her lists that getting elected to various positions did not make her feel respected. Her activities might be very satisfying to someone else. The fact that they did not give her a sense of contentment does not mean that her activities are bad. It merely means that they were wrong for her; if her mother were in her place, *she* probably would be content.

But this woman is not her mother. She is a woman who wants to do something for people. She feels good when she helps others.

Look at that list of goals at twenty-five. This is an excellent example of how material goals increase when you don't do what you really want. The list is full of material "things." Only the last item on the list, sadly enough, is "To be happy." Apparently material things didn't help.

The list of goals at thirty reflects how empty and unfulfilled this woman feels. There no longer is such a great need to please her mother. That drive has lost its strength. She is, however, caught up in so many of the old draining activities (by which she tried to please mother) that she has no energy left for new enterprises. Presently she seems to be avoiding anything that can tax her strength. This woman needs a single goal that will help her direct her energies.

That goal still seems to be a wish to do social work or to work with underprivileged people. This woman has acquired many skills over the years. She has been president of several groups and has much experience in organizing and managing people. She could concentrate her efforts on doing community work perhaps at an organizational level. The dozens of hours a week she spends in committees does not seem to be satisfying to her and is only taking up time and making it more difficult for her to get started on going back to school! or working in the community or whatever. The longer she waits, if you remember, the harder it will be.

What about her mother? Well, thirty-four years of living to please mother is enough, don't you think?

Another useful idea is to make a list of things you can do now that you couldn't do (or had no experience with) when you were twenty. For our young housewife this list might look as follows.

SKILLS AND EXPERIENCE REQUIRED OVER THE YEARS

Know how to manage a meeting
Know how to organize a group project
Know how to get people to work for me
Know how to manage a home
Know how to manage finances
Know how to plan a vacation, trip, day, or year for a family.

I'm sure your list will be even longer and that you will be surprised to discover how much you can do that you never even thought about before. Well, these are real accomplishments! They are real gains, real and valuable skills. It's time you gave yourself credit for all the skills you have.

And there's more. You haven't yet made a list of the things you know now that you didn't know when you were twenty. You'll find that's a long, long list, too. You've got most of the raw materials, more than you are aware of. What you need is *a sense of direction.* Once you know what your goals are, you will find it easier to tell what additional skills and knowledge you may need to get there.

Well, where do you stand? Do you have most of what you want or are you still a long way off? Are you looking in the right direction? Have you been too unrealistic, wanting too much or risking too little?

You May Be Winning More Than You Think

The chances are that, if you have been working hard at the right goal over the years, you will find that you have much of what you claim you still want to win. If that is so, and a large number of readers are going to be surprised to find this is true, then you probably should *stop trying so hard* to reach less important goals. Start enjoying what you have won! *You may already be where you want to be*. You just don't know how to be content with it yet because you haven't weeded out the trivia. Being content begins when you know you have what you want and take time to enjoy it. The right goal is what it takes for you to feel content, whole, at peace with yourself. It is the goal beneath the facade of materialistic glitter.

The law of diminishing returns applies directly to any situation where you are not sure of what you want and try to get more just for the sake of getting more. When "success" is not satisfying, you will find that your needs expand as you get more. After a while it takes a greater effort just to feel that you are not falling backward—like the housewife who kept on joining committees.

There is an optimum size for everything. There is a particular-size home that is just right for a particular wife to manage without having to send out for a straightjacket every afternoon at four. There is an optimum-size business for a particular person that he can handle without running scared. There is a farm just the right size for a certain farmer. The list is endless. As soon as the size of an enterprise becomes greater than a person's natural ability to manage it, his functioning suffers and his anxiety increases. As his expectations rise and his accomplishments fall, his self-image drops. The cycle feeds on itself.

Do You Need More—Or Perhaps Less?

When too much of a good thing doesn't seem to be good for you, cut it back to size, your size. You be the judge. If you have to crowd clients together to meet expenses and you don't like the pace and can't do your best work, you can cut down, become smaller. What do you need all that aggravation for?

Winning is knowing what you need to make *you* happy and achieving it. Not what your parents thought would make you or them happy, not what some movie star or politician needs to be happy. *Only you* can say what your needs are and *only you* can determine whether you need more or perhaps less to make you happy.

When you allow other people (parents, spouses, children, etc.) to make your decisions for you, you permit them to substitute their goals for yours. That may be the way for them to win, but it's not the way for you. You can only lose because no matter how hard you struggle you will not feel fulfilled. You can be happy fulfilling someone else's needs only if both you and the other person are *independently* served by the same action. If you need additional money and you work overtime to get it, you make yourself *and* your boss happy; but to work long hours all the time just to please your boss will drain your own energies. Working hard without considering your real needs will make you a loser.

The size of your real needs, balanced against your ability to work, should determine the number of projects you undertake. It is far better to reduce your goals than to overextend yourself by taking on positions or projects that are beyond your realistic reach. To do so is only a guarantee that one day you will be overwhelmed. Eventually your inadequacy to cope will begin to show up.

It is better to be working slightly under capacity than over it. When you work just below your capacity you have energy left over to manage other people and control your life instead of keeping your guard up for fear of being discovered as a failure. All people who work above their capacity are secretly convinced that they are failures. They're not doing their best and know it. When you work below capacity, you are in better shape; and if you stay focused on your goals you accomplish more, even though you work less your efforts are more on target. You feel relaxed and confident, and you are able to give whatever impression you wish. You will deal effectively with people without fear that at any minute you will be damned as a blockhead—which in time you will be if you get involved in a situation over your head. The moment you lose control of your environment, the moment you have bitten off more than you can chew, you begin to lose control of your destiny and risk being carried away with the tide of your own ambition.

Maybe You'll Do Best To Stay Put

If you do not feel you should move ahead, don't move ahead. If you feel that someone less experienced and less talented than you is willing to move ahead in your place when you don't want to, let him. If he succeeds, you haven't lost anything, providing you've come to terms with what you want. If he does fail, it may be possible for you to move up at your own pace on your own terms later on. Succeeding after refusing to advance in such a situation makes you seem much wiser, as if you had known the move was not prudent.

When you determine what your goals are, you might also discover that you are very far from realizing them. One of the most common reasons for this is that you have diversified—hedged your bets to limit failure—and spread your energies too thin. The more you hedge on failure, the more you diminish your chance for success. It's like a general spreading his troops out to cover the entire front. This leaves him with insufficient strength anywhere to launch a winning push. Guarding too eagerly against failure by spreading yourself too thin always causes failure. As I mentioned before, success depends upon exerting the maximum energy possible toward fulfilling one's goals as soon as practical, once those goals have been decided upon.

Too Many Goals Spoil Your Chances

A person who vacillates among many goals is likely to use up his drive. Some people need many goals because they have unusually active minds and a great deal of energy, but even they need to be restrained and to refocus from time to time.

If you have not achieved your goals because they are too many, separate them into various categories (such as: career, spiritual, recreational) in order to help with the process of sorting. Go by your feelings to determine a new order of importance for these goals and redirect your energies so you will reach the most important ones.

Without goals, your actions are uneconomical, using up more effort than they are worth, leaving you feeling defeated and beaten in the end. When you establish goals firmly in your mind, you change the way you see the world.

When you set goals, you establish new perspectives. Time often makes goals seem clearer. If you look back at the person you once were, you find it a much simpler task to discover where you were, and what you were doing wrong. This is a much more authentic and rewarding view of yourself than you get by looking in the mirror now. Over the years you have developed a sense of who you are, and this gives a point of view that allows you to make the judgments that are right for you. When you establish goals, *you, in effect, place yourself in the future and look back on where you are now*. Setting goals realigns your life in a way that allows you to see what is important. When you set goals, you create, in the present, the same distance that allows you to see the past so clearly.

Setting goals and determining what values are most important to you, what ambitions you can most comfortably handle, are vitally important to winning. Without knowing what your goals are, you will never even know whether you have reached them. And without reaching your goals you cannot be happy, you can never win.

IF YOU DON'T set limits for yourself, you won't get results. Goals are like the steps on a staircase. They tell you where you are going. Limits are like the bannister. They keep you safely on the stairs.

In order for a wife to resume her career teaching modern dance, she must practice a certain number of hours a day and take lessons each week. Although her husband has fears about her becoming involved outside the house, he goes along with her wishes.

The wife did not feel she could be happy spending all her time at home. She felt she was becoming a witch and the world's worst wife to boot. Resuming her dancing seemed to make her feel more complete, more able to give. But it was upsetting to her husband. Every chance her husband has, he tests her limits.

HUSBAND: Uh, Tuesday night next week there's a bowling championship. I'd like to go.

WIFE: I'll make sure you've got a sitter.

HUSBAND (*in apparent total ignorance that she'll be out, too; after all, she's only gone out for the last fifty Tuesday nights in a row*): A sitter?!

WIFE: Dance lessons, remember?

HUSBAND: Don't you think you could stay home, like *other* wives?

She knows she is not going to give away her rights. They were won after a long, hard fight. They are hers. She can talk about them, but always with the understanding that she will keep them. Otherwise she should not even bother to answer.

WIFE: I'm not like *other* wives. I'm me! There's no problem, I'll get a sitter.

HUSBAND: That's going to run into money—with your lessons and all.

WIFE: I pay for my lessons by *giving* lessons, dear, remember? The sitter is your expense, not mine. I babysit for you all week long!

This wife knows what her limits are. She wants a career in dance. She knows what her guidelines are. She has to go to dancing class and to practice regularly. She also knows that some days she doesn't feel like going to dance class and feels disenchanted with it all, but still she sticks to the pursuit of her goal. She is also aware that if she reveals her own occasional doubts about her work, her husband, who always opposed her dancing and still does, will swoop down on her to take advantage of her uncertainty and try to make her quit. If he did get the chance to do so, it would only be because she let him, since she is certainly aware of how he feels.

He would be doing her dirty work if he got her to give up dancing when it was getting difficult for her—providing her with a way out. While you are striving hard to attain a goal, it is almost bound to appear discouragingly out of reach from time to time. You may look for an excuse to quit. It is at this time that the limits you have set vis à vis other people—limits that have allowed you to get as far as you have—are in the greatest danger of being trespassed on.

Trespassers Keep Out!

If the housewife stops asserting her rights and allows her limits to be trespassed on by her husband, she only invites further trespassing later on when she will feel less discouraged and will want to do what she had bargained so long for the right to do. Even if she is convinced that she can't stand on her own two feet, let alone dance, she should be free.

HUSBAND: I get pretty sick of this running in and out, with you never being home.
WIFE: Never? That's not true.

She picks him up quickly on the word "never." In testing limits, testers use words like "never" and "always." That's the way they feel the situation is, not the way it is in reality.

WIFE: . . . that's so exaggerated it's insulting. I won't respond to it.
HUSBAND: You always get your way.
WIFE: Not always . . .

Restate the rules when your rights are threatened. It makes the other person the violator, instead of making you the punisher—and that's hardly a small difference.

WIFE: . . . We agreed that unless you were willing to put me in a mental institution and throw the keys away, I needed a world and an activity of my own. "My own" means exactly that. Mine, something that no one would intrude on. When the kids were really sick and you would have your hands full, I've stayed home, instead of going to class. I just want my share of time. Part of what we agreed on was that you'd stop throwing all this up in my face and try and chisel time away. Remember?

HUSBAND: Yeh. It's a stupid bowling thing anyhow.
WIFE: Go if you want, we'll get a sitter.
HUSBAND: Nah, I'll watch the match on TV.

You see, after all that noise the match was on TV! He was just testing her again. It's like a baby saying "no" before he obeys you.

Without limits, other people will follow their natural bent and go as far as they can. If you wait until then, you may be unable to set effective limits and you may not be able to channel your energies toward your goal.

Limits, both on you and on others, should be reasonable. The husband should not expect his wife to sue for divorce if he makes her miss a class; she should not be inflexible. When limits are too rigid, the goal may get lost. Too much control over people turns them passive and makes them unproductive.

This is especially useful to remember in managing creative people. Creative people need rather wide limits within which to work because the creative process itself is somewhat disorganized. It is difficult to create something new when one is confined by limits that rigidly define who and what you are and should be doing; that way, all you get is a variation of the old.

To set reasonable limits, be certain that the limits help you reach your goal. You should know how much time you wish to invest and how rapidly you wish to move along. Then keep track of how well you are doing.

How to Win at Dieting

The most common form of limit-setting practiced in this country, and one of the least successful, is dieting. What you eat and how well motivated you are is very important, but guidelines that give you feedback make it easier to diet, because you know how you're doing and can correct minor failures before they get out of hand. A simple way of applying this technique to dieting is to buy an accurate scale and to chart each day's or week's weight on a piece of graph paper so that progress can be seen and studied. Another visual guideline is to take a weekly photograph and display it on the refrigerator. This makes sticking to the diet much easier because your progress toward the goal is in clear perspective, and you're constantly reminded of your original intent.

The best limits encourage you to work without demoralizing you. You must be the judge.

Limits are useful in initiating almost all actions and plans: how long you will push a car before you call the tow truck; how many insults you will take before you react; how many minutes you will tolerate an employee being late. Once action is taken, limits can be used to prod yourself to decide how many pages a day you must read or write; how many job applications you will fill out; how many acres you will plant each week. Limit-setting *sets the rate of progress for achieving your plans*. You know when to speed up, just like a truck driver who has fallen behind schedule. Limits are also helpful to *maintain* your goals once you reach them. You need to know when to act to keep your property intact.

How To Break Up the Task

Setting limits is similar to setting and maintaining a pace, as in mountain-climbing. The most helpful limits divide a goal into smaller segments that allow you to approach it step by step. This is very important because, I suspect, some people abandon their goals before they begin—not because they are unable to do what they want, but because they try to do it all at once and are *overwhelmed*. Most people are not disciplined enough to stick with a task, especially when it seems distasteful or unproductive. Discipline is necessary in all large tasks. Your initial enthusiasm may be enough to carry you over some of the rough spots—every undertaking has its exuberant honeymoon stage. The rest is just plain hard work that must be organized and managed, or else it will pile up and get out of control and will swamp you.

Setting limits and deadlines is like pressuring yourself, but if this is done in day-to-day chunks, the amount of work needed to fill the daily quota is surprisingly easy to manage. The final goal becomes approachable. Pressure is great only when no limits are set and the *entire* project looms starkly, waiting to be done.

If you are willing to discipline yourself, you can accomplish a great deal. Want to write but can't get started? This is probably because you look at the total size of the book and worry about all of the thousands of details involved. No wonder you can never get down to business! But if you write three pages a day, four days a week, six months a year, you can write a three-hundred-page book in a year. It's the same with everything else. People tend to forget that every big task is a collection of little tasks.

To *enforce* guidelines is a matter of discipline again. If you have set a minimum amount of time to write each day, make sure you spend all of that time writing. If your quota is a minimum number of pages, you should sit there until you have written them. Good or bad or indifferent, fulfilling your quota is better than losing momentum.

How To Enforce Limits with Others

When another person exceeds your limits, remind him that a violation has occurred and see whether he corrects it. Try to keep things impersonal. Don't say, "*You* did this wrong." Say, "This wasn't done right." Don't make personal accusations; they just enrage others.

To set limits with an employee who arrives late for work, begin by looking at your watch when he looks at you. He'll probably know what you mean. If not, the next step is to restate the limits to the offender: "The day begins at 9:00."

If you can get others to correct themselves, you are best

off. If the limits are still not met or are ignored, the violation must be discussed openly. Ask the violator what *he thinks* should be done rather than take action yourself. This gives him another chance to comply and also reminds him of the consequences. Finally, if this doesn't work, the consequences that you discussed with the violator *must* be enforced. If you don't enforce them, your basis for asserting authority will be eroded and will eventually evaporate.

It is crucially important that the limits you set are vitally related to reaching your specific goals (for instance, eating no more than 1000 calories a day to lose weight). After all, the goal is the only reason to set limits in the first place. To set limits merely to assert your authority, or to make others obey you, will only undermine you. Whether or not a limit should be enforced depends only on whether doing so will help get the job done.

A brilliant contract attorney whose actions have saved his company millions of dollars was fired for breaking trivial limits. He disliked getting up early in the morning and was almost never in his office before ten. He closed his office door, shutting out his associates, when he did arrive so that he could work uninterruptedly. He took a two-hour lunch every day to think, and he left work whenever he felt he was finished. Sometimes this was right after lunch. At other times it was ten P.M. on Saturday when he was the only one in the office. He did what was needed to do his job, and he did it better than anyone else ever had.

As a result of the stifling regimentation that large corporations frequently develop when they are poorly managed, he was reprimanded many times by his supervisor. The supervisor was obviously threatened by the attorney's nonchalance in dealing with company regulations and insisted on making him comply with the rules for their own sake. For this attorney to comply with the company rules would not best serve the goals of the company. To comply with the rules was only in the best interest of the rules themselves. When the lawyer left, the company suffered sizable losses.

Too often, a concern with limits hides a concern with the wrong issue. If the goal is being accomplished, be very careful about enforcing limits. They may be unnecessary, interfere with success, and anger subordinates.

It would have been more useful for the attorney's supervisor to tell him how he upset the office staff; that his fine work was appreciated, but that he should be less disruptive.

Too many large companies seem to consider that obeying rules for their own sake and following standards for dress, hair style, and attitude are more important than productivity. This misdirection is why bureaucracies grow, why committees were invented, and why new ideas and good people get squelched.

Like everything else, companies have an optimum size. Your company has reached its maximum effective size and is about to become a loser when it can no longer discover its brightest people and give them the headway they need to pull it ahead. The most valuable people set their own limits. You do better to consider the goals they accomplished, rather than how closely they adhere to your methods. Maybe their method is better. You can become sidetracked in enforcing limits and forget why they were established in the first place.

When you must enforce a limit, be firm and decisive, but give ample warning beforehand. If someone is not producing, or is trespassing on your territory, give him an opportunity to change. If he doesn't change within a reasonable time (*you* determine how much time is reasonable), you may conclude that he does not want to change or that he does not have the ability to do so. Neither situation is in your best interest. In establishing and enforcing your limits, you have done for him what he could not do for himself. If you have stated the problem clearly, told him what you expected of him, given him time to correct his errors, he will have a clear sense of his failure. He will be able to see what he did wrong and to profit by it. To avoid the truth to protect someone's feelings does more harm than good.

Never Make an Empty Threat

You should never threaten to take a stand when you are not prepared to follow it up with action. Never give an ultimatum unless you have exhausted the alternatives and are willing to carry it out. If you don't act when your terms are not met, your word, authority, and image dwindle in value. You are then regarded as someone who does not need to be taken seriously. You should not take a rigid stand on a trivial issue even if you *are* prepared to follow it through. It just makes you seem unreasonable. And if you find that you are wrong after taking a stand, admit it. You can back down and appear even stronger for being able to do so. But to give an ultimatum, to maintain that you are right and then back down, is self-defeating.

You should know within reasonable limits what it would take to make you happy. You should also establish a point below which you will not accept what is offered to you, be it a minimum salary, standard of behavior, or performance. Unless you have established such a minimum point and are prepared to stick to it, you will find it difficult to win any argument or win any negotiation. You will just lose over and over.

Don't wait until you are backed into a corner to set limits and are at the mercy of others and forced to fight on their terms. If you set a minimum point, you will not need to give away as much. The other fellow's terms are usually losing terms to you.

Winners know when something is not acceptable. When they see that they are not getting what they want, they get out and move to where the odds are better. Although they do not compromise their goals, they accept the fact that every situation has some drawbacks, and that some offer very little chance for success and fulfillment. They learn which situations are likely to help them attain the results they seek and which are not. They will not accept bread today in place of cake, only to be discouraged tomorrow. They accept the realities of the present to avoid losing control of their destiny.

13 / HOW TO MAKE WINNING DECISIONS

YOU WILL PROBABLY make your next big mistake the next time you make a big decision. That's probably when you made the biggest mistakes in your past—picking the wrong job, choosing the wrong school, acting at the wrong moment, buying the wrong business, or buying a house that was too small or too big. Most people, looking back on their mistakes, lament, "If only I'd known more," or "If only I'd had more time to decide, everything would have turned out differently."

There is no way of knowing everything, but there is a way of knowing more before you make your next decision. And there is a way to have more time to *think over* your decision.

First of all, many people fear making decisions because each decision is a venture into the unknown for them. And nothing contributes more to their confusion than not knowing whether a particular decision is important or not. Without knowing this they squander their energy in many directions, worry about countless problems, and end up solving none of them well.

Decision-making seems like flipping a coin when you don't know what you really want. The anxieties of the present crowd you and force you to act on the facts as you see them at the moment. Unfortunately, that moment is too brief to get your bearings or to weigh all the alternatives. Decisions made on the moment are usually the weakest, because they are based only on the facts that are available at the time. That's always bad because the forces that pressure you into making such decisions frequently distort the facts and obscure the truth. While it is true that all decisions are *acted upon* in the present, the best decisions are, in fact, *made* long before.

A decison should reflect your goals. If your goals are clear, your decisions are easy. Without goals you are only guessing.

The best decision for you may not be the most appealing or the one that offers you the most immediate satisfaction. That's what makes this business of deciding so complicated.

Keep in mind that few decisions are ever totally pleasing. Think of the big decisions you've made in your life. They all had drawbacks. Buying a house tied up money that could have been invested in a business. Investing money in a business eliminated a vacation or a hobby. Decisions like this involved postponing pleasure now for larger gains later. The house may have been a good investment and the business may let you take more vacation now. Sometimes avoiding pleasure now and making a sacrifice is the only way of being happy in the long run. Sometimes making a decision that seems less attractive on the surface than its alternatives is the only way you can move along to the next step toward reaching your goal.

Is It a Big One or a Little One?

Before you can make the best decision, you must be able to tell whether it is a major decision or a minor decision. And this again requires that you have a very clear idea of what your goals are. A minor decision has little effect on your goals; a major decision effects them greatly. A major decision deserves your full attention and energy; a minor decision doesn't. Yet it's not always easy to separate a big one from a little one.

Selecting an entree in a restaurant is usually a minor

decision. However, if a girl is on her first date with someone she really likes, the choice of an entree could be important because it influences the impression she makes. She does not, for instance, want to look like a gold digger by choosing the most expensive dish on the menu. She may want to want to show off her French pronunciation to display her general *savior faire*. She'll be careful not to involve the captain in a knowledgeable discussion about the sauce, so she won't seem spoiled or controlling.

Trivial decisions may keep you from thinking about one that is more important, a decision you're avoiding because you fear resolving it. And some deceptively small choices are really major decisions in disguise. Picking an ugly typeface for your company stationery can be offensive to customers you wish to impress. Smoking a competitor's cigarette at an advertising presentation to a tobacco company is a major blunder.

Remember this standard for determining whether a decision is major or minor: how much does it affect your goals? If choosing a band of cigarettes fulfills only your immediate needs, the choice is minor. If choosing the wrong brand may effect the welfare of your family and company, it is a major decision and you should treat it as such.

People who tend to make right decisions will ignore apparently large issues because *they have no great effect on their life*. Yet when they believe a small point can affect them, they act upon it and act quickly. They know what consequences smoking the wrong brand of cigarettes could carry. What is a minor decision to one man, is a major decision to another. Be your own judge; don't depend on what others tell you.

Why It's Easy To Make Bad Decisions

Bad decisions frequently offer short-term solutions to long-term problems. The person making a bad decision may be unaware of the long-term goal or choose the short-term goal because it appears easier—like purchasing an automobile that is cheaper but will require a great deal of upkeep. The low price tag is deceptive.

Many short-term goals are decided upon out of a fear of failure. It is not uncommon to see men settle for jobs beneath their capacity to function—just because they can then avoid working hard. Eventually they wither in this situation because they do not feel challenged and do not grow. Unfortunately, many women find themselves in a similar situation when they give up a career and settle for a role that they come to view as unchallenging and one that has only a limited future. Initially, marriage and a home represented an easy way out for them. Perhaps they felt they would not have to work anymore and that they would find security. They made a decision that shaped their future without considering whether they had personal goals they wished to fulfill. And so they feel trapped in a house of screaming kids and have trouble convincing themselves that their IQ is really over seventy.

The wish not to compete and not to risk exposure also prompts bad decisions. If you accept the idea that you will have to struggle to see your first signs of progress, you will be able to avoid many bad decisions. A decision that appears easier often only postpones the effort to win. If you think hard work is bad and you avoid a choice just because it involves work, you hurt your chances to succeed.

Choices that permit the easy way out are almost always doomed to early failure. Even if your decision seems easy you'll eventually need to work simply because all beginnings require a great deal of effort. If your choice did not suit you, you'll have to work even harder, and you will not be able to move ahead as rapidly as you wanted.

Early in their career when young people make decisions that offer them security they are often not getting a bargain. This is the case with many youngsters who go into their family's business instead of pursuing a native talent. In a few years their lack of interest or natural ability in business begins to show.

Although they have security, they do not feel comfortable or pleased with themselves. In fact because of boredom, decreasing ambition, and a lack of talent in the business, they may actually become failures and may lose all the security for which they compromised. Had they chosen to follow their talent they might have had a rougher time at the beginning, but their interest and ability would have helped them. There's nothing like liking what you're doing to be a success at it.

Don't Let Others Butt In

Bad decisions are often made under the pressure of others. When someone tries to force you to make a decision rapidly, you should see red warning flags go up all around you. Often people make statements to pressure others purely for effect and have no intention of taking action. However, if you take them seriously, they take themselves seriously. People tend to act the way they are reacted to.

If you feel pressured, simply state that you are not sure and that you cannot decide until you settle the issues in your own mind. Even though you feel that by not acting you may risk failure, more often than not it will turn out to be your saving grace.

Learn to take your time with decisions. Ask yourself: "What can I lose by waiting? What can I possibly gain?" You can't always be sure that your decision is right, but it is almost always possible (and almost always a good plan) to take your time deciding.

There may be more involved than meets the eye, especially if you are being pressured to decide about something immediately. Would you be unable to get the same chance tomorrow? If you cannot have the same opportunity in a day or two as now, then it probably has not resulted from your hard work. It comes by chance. If you take such a "golden opportunity" before you are ready, you may be putting yourself in a position beyond your present ability to handle it—and be setting yourself up to fail. Instant glory can become monumental failure—like the fate of the movie star who gets a big break and fails after the first success. Your opportunity will come when you are ready.

When you are pressured into making a decision in a hurry, ask "Why do I have to rush?" You deserve an answer to that question as much as the person pressuring. If you don't get an answer, wait. You probably regret many hasty decisions you made and wonder why you did. Don't make the same mistake again. Think of your decisions over the years. How many good ones did you make on the spur of the moment? How many bad ones?

Once you have made a decision you can act quickly. As I've said: good decision-making is merely acting in response to predetermined goals. It may appear to be rapidly done. But it is not. It is the result of planning, of knowing what you want so that when the time comes, you are ready. If you don't do your homework you'll be confused, in trying to decide at once what your goals, limits, and needs are. It is difficult to think straight with so many confusing issues facing you.

How To Deal With Indecisiveness

People often make decisions because they cannot tolerate indecision. This is especially true of young people entering their twenties. Our society expects its young people to make decisions before most of them have any idea of what they want, and to make plans and implement them. For some people, making any choice at a time of indecision relieves pressure and makes them feel better, even if it is the very worst move they could make. They'll feel worse soon.

Indecision sometimes makes young people feel disorganized. But often, following a period of confusion, it is possible to give up old ideas and prejudices and bring issues into sharper focus. A reordering of goals can result, and decisions can be made in response to the new order. So indecision can be the beginning of a valuable period of growth.

To make an easy decision merely to avoid feelings of self-doubt only buries those doubts temporarily. They will resurface later, in the face of another, more difficult decision. Solving postponed problems requires more energy the second time around. Attempting to avoid big decisions when they appear never works out. The smaller decisions that you handle improperly eventually create bigger decisions that exceed your ability to manage.

Faced with a decision that does not seem clear, and where you cannot decide which alternative is best, you have several choices:

1) You can avoid the problem altogether.

2) You can get more information or more education or take more time to reconsider it.

3) If, after all this, you cannot decide what is best, you can choose the alternative that seems least likely to interfere with your plans. *You can decide what is worst and avoid it.*

Just because a decision will not make you happy does not mean it is the wrong one. Since no decision makes everyone happy, you must decide only if reaching your goal is made more possible through your decision.

If you do not know what your goals are—don't decide.

Almost nobody really likes to fight, but almost everybody does! So it's in your best interest to know how to defend yourself.

Almost everyone is afraid of expressing angry feelings and getting yelled at in return. It *is* unpleasant to confront other people sharply, but sometimes it's impossible to avoid. Angry feelings grow when you try to conceal them. Even if you don't know why you're angry, you're aware of feeling uneasy when an opportunity to get angry presents itself.

No one likes losing control of his temper or playing the bad guy who hurts other people. Yet if you express your anger when someone hurts you, it seems appropriate. You get it out of your system and do not feel the need to seek revenge. When you let anger build up, it tends to destroy you by consuming your valuable time and energy.

You can learn to have an argument without losing control of yourself and win something for yourself to boot. In a good argument both sides can win by resolving the painful feelings between them.

What To Do Before Getting into an Argument

Before getting involved in an argument, consider this simple energy-conserving question: *"Could I be wrong?"* Try to prove that you are wrong with as many different approaches as possible. *That's exactly what the other guy will do to you!* If you decide you are wrong, perhaps the argument would be best handled by simply avoiding it. If you can't find a single reason why you might be wrong, you could be in big trouble because you're just not looking hard enough.

Next, do your best to look at the argument from the *other* person's point of view. Consider what kind of person he is, what you know of his actions in the past, and what his goals are.

Now compare your case with his. Try hard to be objective! Very often, the question of whether it is worthwhile to have an argument is best decided by going no further than this stage.

Let's suppose that you want to have a showdown and believe you are right—and that it's important to make the other person, a cantankerous man, see your side. Consider his personality: rigid and bitter. Is it possible to win an argument with him and make your point, or will any argument alienate him, so that, even if you win, you will lose? It is his rigidity that made you so angry in the first place. Rigid people are difficult to deal with, and you'll feel even angrier the more contact you have with them. You must decide in this light whether having an argument is worth it or not. If it's probably not worth it, avoid it; it's only bound to bring you more grief. Rigid people won't even be touched by you—you're no more than a nuisance to them.

The best way to fight any argument is to do what is necessary to prevent the original conflict from occurring in the first place. That means you should have pointed out your differences when they were small, when pointing them out would not have been upsetting to either party. But it's too late now, you say. There's an argument lurking around here somewhere, just waiting to take place.

Before you get involved, ask yourself, "What am I really

angry about?" "Am I angry at him or disappointed with my-self?" Remember: it's easy to become angry at your own fail-ures and to feel that it's necessary to blame them on others. When you try to blame others, your arguments eventually ap-pear very weak. Your inconsistency will be noticed by others, even if they don't mention it. Since blaming others is common to everyone, it is important that you recognize it and that you be willing to admit it when it is brought up. If you deny what is obvious, you appear foolish. If you admit it, you disarm the other party and can concentrate on your stronger points.

Here's the Wrong Way and the Right Way

With your goals in one hand and your knowledge of your own mistakes and contribution to the difficulties in the other, you are prepared to move into action. Let's watch two business partners argue.

RON: Everything's going wrong. Money isn't coming in, the bills are overdue.

ED: So what else is new?

RON: Dammit, you don't take anything seriously! Why aren't sales better? Why aren't we pushing harder?

ED: It seems to me that we are both responsible for running the company . . .

RON: So you had to go and take a vacation just now?

ED: It was the dullest time of the year. I always take vacations in August. There's never any business. Would you rather I took one in October?

RON: But this August is worse than ever.

ED: What do you want me to do about it?

Ed has asked for a specific complaint. Up to this point he has viewed Ron's comments as representing the usual discontent with business that the two of them frequently have during dry seasons. But listen to a new turn now:

RON: I think you could take more of an interest in the company.

This was exactly the wrong statement to make. Although Ron feels that more effort from Ed would be useful, he has phrased it with such anger (insinuating that Ed doesn't have any real interest in the company) that he has alienated Ed.

ED (*flushing*): What is that supposed to mean?

Again Ed is asking for a specific issue.

RON: You could spend more time with the salesmen. You could call on the accounts and see why they don't pay.

ED: Are you trying to tell me that there is something wrong with the way I run the sales operation?

RON: Well, all I know is that we're not selling.

This is a good point for Ron, because it brings out a point of fact which Ed must explain, rather than calling Ed a bad sales manager.

ED: Ron, what's the matter with you? You know this is a crappy month. Why is it you only comment about crappy months? If you take a close look at the earnings you'd see that all the bad months are seasonal.

Everyone is happy when sales are good, unhappy when they are bad. Could Ron have avoided this argument?

RON: Well, a good salesman can sell in any month.

ED: Don't pull that crap with me, Ron. That's the kind

of tactic I take with my salesmen. I'm your partner . . . what's bothering you? I'm as upset about the company not doing well as you are. I'm doing my best.

RON: Well, do something. . . .

ED: Like what? I've screamed at the salesmen. I've made dozens of calls myself. No one's going to buy anything until late September.

RON: And you believe that?

ED: I believe the figures we've accumulated over the last ten years.

RON: Well, you should have a new tactic.

Ron is too vague, pushing too hard.

ED: What about your creating some new products? They've all seen our stuff before. The salesmen need something new to show the customers. And that's *your* department. Hey, why aren't *you* doing something?

Ron finds this turn of events is unexpected. Now Ron is on the defensive and is beating a retreat back to his drawing board. The final result may turn out to be best for the company because both partners may work harder. The situation could have been handled with much less emotional wear and tear if Ron had begun with an appeal to Ed to see how business could be improved, instead of launching a personal attack. Ron may feel too defeated to give his best effort and he may have lost Ed's cooperation.

Here's another argument—this one between a husband and wife over finances, children—anything they can get their hands on. See if you can determine what the real concerns of each spouse are and how the argument could have been conducted better. The uncontrolled anger leaks through (and is italicized).

SHE: This is the absolute limit! *You try* to carry every last bit of dirt in from the street and *mess up this house. You don't care* how hard I work.

HE: What are you *yapping* about again?

Up to now, the only point that has been made is that both are angry.

SHE: Look at your *big* feet. Look at that mud. What do we have a mud room for?

HE: I don't know . . . it was another of your *brilliant ways* to spend my money.

SHE: What's that supposed to mean? *You're the brilliant one* who doesn't know enough to wipe his feet. . . .

This kind of argument wins prizes for its stupidity and pointlessness. It becomes an insult-match.

HE: Forget it! Is supper ready?

SHE: I only have *two hands* and you look like you could do *without* a meal now and then (*poking his belly with broom handle*). Must be jelly 'cause jam don't shake like that!

HE: I guess *we all* begin to lose our shape after a while.

SHE: How'd you like supper in the garage?

HE: Speaking of the garage, do you have any idea what that door cost to be repaired?

So that's what he's angry at!

SHE: If I don't now, I soon will, won't I, dear?

HE: You're right *for once.* You certainly will. One hundred and twenty-eight dollars.

SHE: You were taken!

HE: And not just by the carpenter! By the minister, too!

SHE: You want to trade me in with the car?

HE: It's not a bad idea! You don't ever look where you go. You could've avoided that accident.

SHE: Why did you wait all this time to yell at me? You were such a perfect gentleman when I hit the door. Was it because you didn't want to appear like the bastard you are in front of the neighbors? I wouldn't want anyone to think that you weren't a sweetie pie, sweetie pie.

HE: No, it was because you were still at the wheel of that damn thing and I was afraid you'd run me over!

If you couldn't tell what the argument was about from the beginning, don't be upset. Family arguments like this can go on for days without either of the parties knowing what they're really angry about. The husband appeared to understand when she had the accident; he buried his anger at his wife. She began to feel guilty about the accident and was looking for an excuse to fight so that they could get off their chests what was bothering both of them. It is unlikely that either of them was aware of anything except a lot of anger floating around, not attached to anything in particular.

At the first excuse they fight. In time the real issue surfaced. Everything would have been much simpler if they had expressed their feelings at the time of the accident, rather than letting them grow out of proportion. No one wins arguments like this, but this couple would have lost less by discussing their feelings earlier.

How To Lose an Argument for Sure

The best way to lose an argument is not to know beforehand what kind of person you are dealing with and not to understand what he wants. Here is an argument between a competitive student and his passive and controlling teacher over an exam grade. This one may sound familiar.

STUDENT: Sir, I would like to discuss my paper with you.

PROF: Yes. . . . (*passive and cool*) By all means!

STUDENT: I think my grade should be higher.

PROF: Yes, I agree. I also believe you are capable of better work.

This kind of answer should put you on guard. It is generated from deep down in the professor's personality. He does not think for a moment that the student's grade could be too low as a result of his unfair marking. He believes he is fair, within his own system. His fairness, his system, is an issue never to be challenged, at least not directly.

STUDENT: I believe my answer in Part II gives all of the effects of Charlemagne's rule.

PROF: No one knows for certain even yet what all of the effects of Charlemagne's rule were. Come, what is your point?

STUDENT (*in the tone of the new-student-left-revolutionary, which he has recently been trying on for size*): I believe I have a right to have Part II reconsidered. I believe I should have received at least five more points, which would have given me at least a B-minus.

PROF (*in the passive-angry, never-yet-having-been-gotten-the-better-of-by-a-student tone which has been his life style these forty years*): Very well! I believe you do have a right. I shall not only review Part II, but I shall reconsider your examination from the beginning as if it had no marks on it whatsoever. You may have earned an additional point here or there. I may also have awarded points where they were not due. We all make mistakes, and I know you want exactly what you deserve!

STUDENT (*realizing that when the exam comes back he will be lucky to have received a pass*): Gulp!

Arguments invariably open up much wider areas of conflict than one originally intends. When anger is unleashed it always finds a target. The student did not know what the teacher had to lose. He didn't take enough trouble to size up his opponent. He could have found out by asking any upperclassman. Besides, if this teacher yields on this point, he risks being deluged by other students and wasting his time in similar arguments. It is never a matter of just a few points. This teacher does not admit he was wrong easily, and when he does, others have to pay a price. You *win* an argument with a teacher like this *by avoiding* it altogether. Those people who pride themselves on being fair can do you in very nicely, especially if *you* are not being totally honest.

If you do know what you want and what the other person is like but you believe it is possible to win an argument that will significantly help your cause, here are some useful tactics to think about.

It is very important to know when to keep your mouth shut. When you are unsure of your point and believe that the other person may be able to refute you, don't make it. It can only make you more unsure, more anxious. Some people win arguments by taking advantage of their opponent's anxiety. So you only invite disaster by opening a subject you are unsure of. You would do much better to keep quiet and to give the other fellow a chance to reveal his weakness. Why should you be the only fool?

How To Start an Argument

Don't begin an argument by announcing the fact. Simply describe the present situation.

BOSS: George, I notice that the department is having problems.

The Boss has not identified the problems specifically yet, because he is interested in learning everything he can. George doesn't know which problems the Boss is referring to, but he knows the problems that exist. If the Boss can remain silent, he will discover more about them than if he asked directly. Asking a specific question at the beginning, would limit George's response.

GEORGE: What are you referring to?

This is George's best move because he is trying to make the Boss commit himself to a specific question so that he doesn't have to reveal his hand, trying to guess which of the many current problems the Boss has in mind.

BOSS: The department has problems with production. The output is below the level we agreed would be acceptable.

The Boss acts under the assumption that George will tell him what's wrong and tries not to give him a way out.

People usually know what they've done wrong, and, given enough time, they will reveal it. They also believe that you know what's wrong even when you don't. Don't let on that you don't.

GEORGE: It's not good; costs just keep climbing. The men today . . . well, you know how independent they are. You tell them something and you have a work protest on your hands.

The Boss interrupts George at this point because he is being too general. He wants concrete details to evaluate. He does not want to allow George off the hook by permitting a bland generalized confession that bad times could be better, that they are the fault of others, allowing George to go away without telling him enough of what is wrong so it can be fixed. If you can't win an argument, you should at least have learned something about what was wrong, either to fix the mistake or to avoid it in the future. If nothing else, you should learn what made you angry in the first place and settle those angry feelings.

BOSS: Well, what do *you* think the specific difficulties are?

The Boss asks for George's opinion in a tone of voice that suggests that he has his own ideas of what is wrong.

GEORGE: I think the machinery is too old for the work load we're demanding.

BOSS: Well, it had the same work load last month and seemed to do fine. Did you try to distribute the work over the light as well as the heavy times of day?

The Boss has asked the question, "Are you managing efficiently," but in a way that is both very specific and indirect.

GEORGE: Well, it's hard with many of the men being new—they need more supervision.

George has revealed a new problem—the effects of the high rate of employee turnover. The Boss can now investigate this new and interesting finding. He should look for reasons for the increase in turnover, ask George to try to define the problem and then offer help in leading George to the solution. He should remain open-ended in his conversations and not make statements that are denigrating or insulting. Blanket statements such as, "It's your job to keep the men working," or "You've solved problems like this before," are suitable for the time being. The object is for both the Boss and George to profit by the encounter.

The Boss should not reveal his personal anger or disappointment. It only gets in the way and puts employees on the defensive. It's okay to show anger with friends, but it is rarely helpful with employees. If you must show anything, show fairness.

The Boss should not allow himself to become a target unnecessarily. When he wants something done, he should frame his requests in terms that make *the company, not him*, the demanding party. Instead of saying, "I'd like you to do this," it is better to say, "the company's success depends on how we distribute the work load." This is more likely to be responded to gracefully. It promotes a sense of a group goal, rather than a feeling of resentment against a dictator. And it is far less argumentative.

When past errors are uncovered during an argument, their discovery alone is usually enough to change the course of events and lead to such possible solutions as getting more data, consulting experts, getting more help or more machines, exerting more energy and effort. Once the problem is noted, the boss should express concern that it does not return.

Several weeks after their argument, the Boss approaches George.

BOSS: George, I see that there are still some problems.
GEORGE: Yes, I'm aware of them. (*He lists them.*)
BOSS: Perhaps we should discuss the situation in a few weeks if it doesn't improve. I'm sure you can handle it.

Some people almost seem to hang themselves when they get into arguments. In fact, they often feel that they need to. They usually can be recognized by their eagerness to concede points, rather than a willingness to disagree with you. You would be wise to give them enough time to confess their errors and accept blame. But don't let them go too far and launch into breast-beating. Intervene and save their face. They'll appreciate it. There's no use in letting someone demoralize himself. That will always work against you, because he will feel that his confession has absolved him of any need to make good.

Always state the problem in impersonal terms. Describe an event as "going wrong," not as someone "messing up." The others know what you mean, but will be less threatened if you are oblique, and will tell you more and be better able to correct their mistakes.

When you have an important point to win and want the other person to follow it, the best way of dealing with the situation may be not to appear to win. Winning an argument is not always walking away with the other fellow's feeling crestfallen and believing that you are the debating wizard of the Western world and that he is a perfect idiot. This is childish and useless and boring, unless it's the way you get your kicks.

What If You Can't Win?

If an argument is going against you and you cannot see how to win, it is best to remain silent for a while and look for a way of getting out of it without making your position worse.

It is to your advantage to concede a weak point to your opponent and then move to a stronger one. Don't bring up your own weak points to defend them, but only to concede them. To do so deflates your opponents, by stealing their thunder.

Take your opponents' best argument, admit it, but treat it as if it were insignificant.

When you have won what you want, you have two options: to end the argument or to continue. You should be cautioned about pushing for too much because even the most pliable person has limits. By being outrageous in your demands you make him realize that he has not been fighting hard enough and is giving in too much, and the lamb may turn into a tiger.

You will have won once you made your point. Only a fool is interested in humbling another person. Expressing too much anger will make you the villain. Let the other fellow go away feeling that he has won *something*. It works out better for you.

If you are close to your goals, it's best to become less active in arguing. This creates tension in your opponent, and he will respond by trying to make the first move toward ending the argument, closing the sale, or concluding the agreement.

Best advice: quit while you're ahead!

15 / CRISIS: THE BEST TIME TO ACT

CHAOS IS YOUR biggest ally, if you know how to use it. If you wish to put chaos to your use, you still must know what you want. You still must have goals and be prepared to take risks to reach them. The advantage of acting in chaos is that others are in a state of disorganization, confusion, or pandemonium.

The techniques discussed in this chapter apply to taking charge of a group of people when they are under stress, not for managing an individual in personal difficulty. The difference in handling these two problems is considerable. Individuals need and deserve attention to their own personal needs. Their sense of worth or their lovability need to be reaffirmed. But when a group is in a crisis, it is disorganized and has a different need. It needs a leader. It needs to be led, not understood.

If you have been watching the crisis develop, you have a sense of cause and effect. If you seem to be the only one who can move in a particular direction, who really knows what he wants, and if you appear cool and clear-headed in all the confusion, you will be able to reason more logically than those caught up in the turmoil of the moment—and that makes all the difference. *Your goals have given you distance, and your distance gives you power.*

What happens to people in a crisis? In a crisis, people are afraid they are going to lose their security, their job, their marriage, esteem, love, or control. They are afraid someone will notice that their short cuts and side dealings have contributed to the present disaster. They are afraid of losing what they consider important and will support the person who appears best able to prevent this and save their face.

In a crisis, people also feel *powerless and childlike*. They need someone to give them direction. Just as adolescents cannot tolerate indecision and often make choices merely for the sake of having a purpose, people in a crisis will move toward leaders who seem the most confident or who give the appearance of knowing what to do.

Crisis: The space which the Woman's Club counted on for the spring charity show has been cancelled. Mrs. White never liked the choice of space. She has many other ideas, including taking over the leadership of the club.

MRS. A: You'd think that people would be decent.

MRS. B (*panicky*): I don't know what to say!

MRS. F: The poor children who benefit from the show drive! What will they do?

CHAIRMAN: Ladies, this is a serious problem. I'm afraid we'll just have to cancel. I've looked elsewhere. There just aren't any other places available.

MRS. A: No! We can't do that!

MRS. B (*shouting*): It's not right!

MRS. WHITE: I have contacted a friend whose husband has a huge hall that we can use. I once considered it for the show, but we seemed so locked into the auditorium. I'm sure I can get it even at this late date.

MRS. A: Yes, get it! Good idea!

MRS. B: Good thinking.

MRS. WHITE: I think we have to find new ways to do a lot of things around here. This organization depends on people who just aren't reliable.

CHAIRMAN: Well, I think that's absurd.

MRS. WHITE: Well, you refused to look elsewhere. Maybe you could have looked harder instead of tying this group in with such an unreliable plan.

CHAIRMAN: Unreliable, my foot! We've had the show the last ten years! You call that unreliable?

MRS. WHITE: If you had looked at the auditorium schedule, you would have seen that they were pressed for space, and the very first thing they would do would be to cut out charity. And they did. That possibility occurred to me last month. That's when I spoke to my friend. There are other suggestions I could make, but they can wait till we settle this business.

MRS. A: Let's hear them now!

MRS. B: Right on!

In a crisis people frequently look for someone to blame, and if they need a scapegoat badly enough they will find it. If you act too rashly, *you* may become it. You can avoid this by showing the others that you have the same goals in common.

Chaos presents opportunities to move ahead which no other situation offers. The leadership of others is at its weakest level of influence. Now is the best time to act with a sense of authority and to present your opinion in the most favorable light. If you have been aware of the events that led up to the present difficulty, your analysis of the situation is needed now. Make yourself known.

What do you say if the others ask why you were silent till now, or why you didn't reveal your plans before this mess developed? Tell them that until now those who were in charge would have found your plans threatening; they would have found fault with them and put them down and destroyed them, just to stay in power.

Don't Move Until Your Plan Is Set

Moving before your plans have been completely worked out can be flirting with danger. Tell colleagues about your plans too soon and you may be inviting them to try to destroy them. People have an irrational loyalty to established leadership and are reluctant to mutiny, (which is the way they will see your plans). Your associates may turn you in to put themselves in a better position with the leader, or they'll squelch any plan of yours that scares them.

But if disorder strikes and you are sure of your ideas, you can act. The others will respect you for discovering who is at fault and will be grateful that you have not blamed them. They will feel purged of their mistakes and will flock to your support. But remember: you must have something to follow your opening act. Many leaders don't. They just repeat the slogans that were successful in allowing them to take over—and then they falter and lose.

During times of confusion, people are plagued with ambivalence and their self-confidence is low. If you are already in charge of a business or any group of people and a sudden disaster overtakes you, you must act to prevent someone else from trying to take over and from upsetting your plans.

To restore confidence in your leadership, begin by admitting that the catastrophe exists. Everyone else is already aware of it and you'd only look like a fool if you tried to deny it. Explain the facts of the crisis as simply as you can—if you can do so without weakening your position. Then give your plans for leading them out of the crisis. If there *is* no clear-cut solution at the moment, point that out, but be sure to indicate that you are certain that there is a way out. State explicitly that you are *committed* to finding it.

If you can't avoid the blame, accept it. The others will know perfectly well that you were not responsible for everything that went wrong, especially the part that they screwed up themselves. Besides, by admitting responsibility for the crisis, you disarm those who would do you in. If you must blame others for the crisis, you should discharge them because you must dispel the doubts of those who remain and show that you believe in what you say. If those to blame are kept in their role, your leadership is less believable.

What To Do About Your Fears

Again, if you have fears, keep them to yourself, or else they will become the target for the criticisms and protests and doubts of others. Do not minimize the struggle ahead to those who must work with you, because they will be easily discouraged at the first setback following a crisis; and then you'll lose their confidence—just when you need it most.

In a crisis, you may be able to consolidate the plans and ideas that you were never able to get started on before. The person who resolves the uncertainty of others in a crisis receives their allegiance and their best efforts. Do not back away from a crisis. It can be your golden opportunity.

A note of caution: a crisis should be used to implement decisions made before—not to make them. Decisions *formed* during a crisis do not usually consider long-range goals and are therefore likely to backfire. But decisions made under fire also appear to have more thrust and power behind them than decisions made at less pressured times, and may therefore seem particularly compelling.

In the confusion of a crisis, actions are sometimes taken that are irreversible—quitting your job, making libelous accusations, sabotaging your marriage—but at such a turbulent time it's best to keep options open. Chaos is an excellent atmosphere for stating your plans in a way that can give them the greatest acceptance and chance for implementation, but not for weighing delicate alternatives.

It is very risky to go out of your way and *precipitate* a crisis in order to achieve your goals. If you can correct the faults without creating a crisis, this is vastly preferable, especially when you are already in charge. The danger in precipitating a crisis is that once it has begun you are committed to act in order to come out on top. Once you've made your move you cannot permit the situation to deteriorate without attempting to take over, because you will eventually be blamed if things go sour. And if that happens before you are in a situation of power and well on the way to correcting the previous faults by your own methods, you will be the one to suffer most.

WHEN PEOPLE act helpless, controlling, or competitive, they are more likely to get in your way and spoil your chances for success.

It is not difficult to manage people in a relaxed situation, but managing individuals when they are under stress can be exasperating. Unfortunately the time when people need to be managed most is usually when they are indeed under stress, for it is then that these troublesome qualities show most. Under stress, people become rigid just when you want them to be most flexible. Usually a person's characteristic way of reacting stays the same even though stresses change. If a man acts helpless when his boss finds fault with him, he is likely to act helpless when arguing with his wife. When he is not under stress he may appear no different from anyone else. This differs from a crisis where a *group* of people are under stress. A group in a crisis feels collectively helpless and is, as I will show later, looking for someone to take charge.

Some people act helpless, controlling, or competitive almost all the time. It is not only their reaction to stress; it's the way they react to life. These character types represent an enlargement of the usual reaction to stress. By understanding them it is possible to learn to deal with people who act similarly only when under stress.

This chapter will show you how to recognize these three character types and the sort of problems each creates, and how to manage them. Once you recognize any person's reaction as helpless, controlling, or competitive you can apply the principles outlined here to manage them. A person who acts helpless only under great stress and a person whose style is to act helpless most of the time are both handled in exactly the same way. You will find people easier to deal with because you will be responding to the needs that are most important to them.

In order to manage another person you must pay him in the coinage of his realm, not in your own. Although it is always easier for you to pay in the currency of your own emotional life, it just is not as meaningful to other people; they will feel cheated and hurt and may undermine you. In their eyes, they will feel justified because they are getting nothing in their currency. A lavish gift may not be worth as much as an accepting and supportive comment at the right time.

The Helpless-Dependent Character Type

This person has an exaggerated concern for being loved, and with the dependability of other people. He tends to see other people as sources or as consumers of supplies. He also tends to be passive in the face of stress. He feeds on reassurance. His actions seem always to depend on other people. Here is a boss with a new employee.

Episode 1:
BOSS: Have you made any progress with that problem?
RICK: Uh, well. You didn't tell me it was that hard. I started to go to the library and it was difficult to find the material. They didn't seem to have much material. *No one was there to help me out.*
BOSS: But what have you done about it?
RICK: Well, *you didn't seem very interested* in the in-

formation, so I figured it wasn't all that important, *if it wasn't important enough for you* to ask again.

    BOSS: Why didn't you come to me?

    RICK: *You didn't ask me to.* So I figured you didn't want me to.

The italicized comments signal the dependent person's wish to be helped or given to; to have an interest shown in himself; and to be considered important. Phrases that reflect these dependent characteristics are present in everything these people say.

    Rick, like many dependent people, is emotionally like a child who needs frequent instruction and leadership. Whatever his abilities may be intellectually, they do not overcome his dependent needs and do not allow him to be successful on his own. Rick needs a constant relationship with another person, usually one who is in charge or in a parental role. He functions best in a passive relationship to others.

Make a Mistake and Risk a Rejection

    If the boss had been aware of this, he would never have made the mistake of asking Rick to start a project without arranging for regular follow-up and supervision. Rick would do well if he were told how to go about each step. Rick is afraid of making a mistake and being rejected because of it. He is not likely to initiate (or carry through) a long project on his own without the emotional investment of other people in his efforts, their support, and their reassurance. He needs to be coaxed and to be praised for his goodness, step by step. In short, *he needs to feel loved.*

    You say you don't want to love him? Then don't hire him and save both of you the misery.

    A key statement should be delivered at the beginning of any arrangement with a dependent type. It should then be repeated and adapted to fit the context of the moment. It should express interest and an offer to help and be reassuring. The boss might have told Rick:

> It's a difficult task, but I know you can do it. Even if you can't, don't worry. You can always come to me for help.

To win with people like Rick, plan a regular time to meet with them when they can discuss their problems with you. They are their own biggest enemies and, if given the chance, will spend all their time tying you up with increasingly childish questions, acting passive and helpless. You must draw a fine line with such types. Although they need to know that you are interested in them and believe in them and like them, they also need just enough push to deploy their intellectual skills, and enough limits to know that you mean business. Set limits, deadlines, and quotas and be sure you both agree on them *beforehand*.

If you have a dependent, passive spouse, be prepared to give emotional support and understand that he/she does not function best independently. Be certain that you show interest in a concrete and understandable way. Be especially careful not to forget birthdays or the anniversaries that your spouse considers important. Remember: even though your spouse is an adult, emotionally she will be injured as if she were a child when the tokens of appreciation (which she deems important) are not offered.

Don't Express Your Doubts

Don't express your self-doubts to a dependent person. It only makes him anxious and unsure of your leadership. He will try to test your strength, your rules, your love. Remember that dependent people look for guidelines and will probably push you until they get them. When they cannot find these guidelines, they may become passive and withdrawn. They may even panic.

Their passivity can be irritating, annoying, and obstructing. They just sit down on the job and expect you to have all the answers—*just as children do* when they feel overwhelmed.

It is easy to tell *who* these people are. You have already met them; you may just not have known *what* they were.

Very often a dependent person is able to do excellent work when given the benefit of the doubt and reassured—told that he can do better and encouraged to try. All this reassuring should be done in a warm, accepting tone. Dependent people make very loyal workers, friends, and spouses. They seldom initiate independent action, although they sometimes do when they sense a serious threat to the person they care about.

They tend to be possessive in their relationships. They easily get discouraged but also respond easily to warmth. They often resent the fact that they need to be treated in this child-like way. So if you overreact and treat them too much like children, you may produce a reaction opposite to the one desired. They may assert that they have no need to be taken care of and initiate rebellious action that ends in failure.

Remember: dependent people recognize that they are lacking something. They also know they want to be *given* a great deal. You should point out that you will try to help them get what they want, but that they will also have to do the work.

Above all, do not try and change them. It can't be done. Just manage them and help them to continue growing.

Although these people make excellent followers, they can assume limited authority for a specific task if it is delegated to them. Dependent people are likely to respond to those in their charge by saying, "The boss told me to tell you to . . ." rather than using their own authority. They need the protective shield of someone else's authority, because they cannot take charge for very long without depleting their sense of personal strength. That strength comes from others. If they need reassurance, they often become overly concerned with what those around them are thinking. Remember, they tend to become passive when they feel threatened and may let problems slide and then feel so guilty and shamefaced about it that they will not be able to talk over their failures with you. Resist the temptation to put these people down! It will only make them act more helpless, which is what you're trying to correct. Your job is to reassure them.

The Controlling Type

The person concerned with control often has a problem that may seem strikingly different from that of dependent people. In fact, his problem may seem like a solution for the dependent person. He is too independent—almost as if it were a reaction formed against being dependent. He does things *his* way.

People who are concerned with control get caught up with little details, the small parts of larger problems. In doing so, they often miss the big picture. They tend to place everything into little compartments. They worry. They worry if something is good. Or bad. Or active. Or passive. Or masculine. Or feminine. They want to know *all the possibilities, all the rules of the game*. They prefer to do whatever they do in neat and orderly ways. While they can be very efficient, the system that they have developed may become so cumbersome and rigid as to obstruct them; it makes achieving their goals nearly impossible.

Beneath the surface, they fear losing control of their own anger and have a nagging doubt that they may be no good, angry, dishonest, or dirty. They are often stuffy, pompous, pedantic, wordy, and so much caught up in logic that they do not seem to have common sense.

Episode 2: The boss and a controlling person (again, typical phrases are italicized).

BOSS: Have you . . .

KARL: Ah. Excellent that you've come by—I have something interesting to show you. I've been looking at that problem. It's quite *complicated*.

BOSS: It seemed straightforward to me!

KARL: Well, I have found almost twenty different solutions which I am trying to narrow down. But *it takes time to research all the details.*

BOSS: Well, let's discuss it. Why haven't you come earlier?

KARL: *I wasn't ready then.* I'm almost complete now. *I've got to get all of the pieces to fit.*

BOSS: What have you decided?

KARL: Well, it's very complicated. There are eight *categories* of products . . . each is two *grades.* I have it all down.

BOSS: I can help you. I've got experience with that. I've been in this for years.

KARL: *I'm not sure I'm finished.* There are a *few more details.*

BOSS: But I need the information.

KARL: Well, I won't have it for a while, not *until I'm satisfied that I'm right.*

Within the week, Karl will present a portfolio of detailed information, much of it off the point. It will be difficult to know what the original question was. The boss will be angry at all the wasted time. Karl will feel unappreciated and much less willing to relinquish his information in such a hurry next time. Karl feels he isn't finished, that he rushed the job, and that to do things properly he must take time and be orderly.

A Mountain of Effort for a Molehill of Details

The Karls of this world eat up billions of dollars in useless research or in paperwork. They are the housewives who buy dozens of spices that they will never use, just to have a symetrically filled spice rack; or who can't go to sleep without washing and putting away every dish in the house. Details! *Their details will drive you crazy!* But only when their details are in order will they feel in order.

Some controlling people choose a place for themselves with a small account ledger in a little office, balancing figures. It is a peaceful haven in which to spend their lives while keeping numbers in order. Others may become exacting school teachers who do not fully appreciate their students' individuality (or their right to learn at their own pace). These people tend to be self-centered and concerned only with their own welfare. They are *unaware* of others' feelings and don't wish to injure intentionally. They are *insulated* against other people's distress, although they themselves feel considerable guilt and envy. They like situations to go their own way all the time and are hesitant to allow others to do something which they feel they could do better themselves. They have lost much flexibility in life. It is so important for them to function in an orderly manner that they find it difficult to make compromises.

But they *do* function. In fact, without traits of this sort of character, there would be very little accomplished in the world. Controllers are people who can organize details into systems and make the systems go. They deal with "things" and make "things" work. Unfortunately, they also have a tendency to see people as "things." Other people resent being treated that way and demand that the controllers be more affectionate and warmer, more spontaneous. To do so is upsetting to controllers; it makes them feel they are losing control.

Controlling people are sometimes good at managing others when they can act with authority, especially absolute authority, as in the military, where they can defer to a strict code of rules. However, when they act as the authority, they often infuriate those around them because they adhere so strictly to rigid rules and demand obedience to them. To be the best kind of manager or administrator, it is necessary to be authoritarian at times. To do so rigidly, as controlling people often do, without a feeling or knowledge of what makes other people function, almost always spoils the effort. These people *can* learn to take other people's feelings into consideration even if they do not understand them. They can learn to react to others on a purely intellectual level.

To try to win with a person like this is more difficult than dealing with any other kind of person, it could easily lead to a collision because both of you are trying to get control over the situation.

The first rule, therefore, is: *don't argue and attempt to show who is in control.* You're just a pale amateur in comparison to this sort of person. He has been fighting for control all his life and knows all the tricks. Well, almost all the tricks.

He Won't Give Up!

So instead of asserting yourself directly, try to get him to use his control in ways that are useful to you rather than to relinquish it. Why? Because he won't give up his control. Don't try to make him. Try to redirect his energies so they will meet your needs. Show him in what ways your goals are similar. Try not to appear as an outraged victim who has been injured by this person's rigidity, but rather as a helpful person who sees an important detail that has been missed.

Remember: to overlook a critical point is a signal to these people that their system is not working; pointing that out will make them feel very unsure. Since your system picked up the detail they missed, they suspect it might work better, that you have the magic touch. They will be looking for faults in your system in order to feel better. Therefore, the less you say to them, the better.

Demand to See the Forest, Not the Trees

BOSS: Well, where's the answer? What price should I quote?

KARL: I don't have it yet.

BOSS: It's too bad. It looks as if we'll lose the account. (*Meaning: Things are out of control.*)

KARL: But I'm working hard at it.

BOSS: I have to decide tonight. That account's important. You're working hard, but at the wrong thing.

KARL: Why didn't you tell me?

BOSS: You said *you* could handle it. You said you knew what was important.

KARL: But it's complicated. So many factors.

BOSS: You should have known that. There are only three items to cost! (*Meaning: Your system should have been able to handle it.*)

KARL: I'll sort out the details right away.

BOSS: Would you like me to tell you which three items *I* had in mind? I need the results and I need them now!

The boss does not comment about any of the particular details of Karl's system. He only implies that the system is not working because the job is not getting done. Karl's goal is to maintain the integrity of the system. The boss's goal is to get the information he needs. He does this by making Karl prove his system works by solving the problem—the way the boss wants it solved.

Whenever you argue over individual details with a controlling person you will almost certainly lose. He has already worked out every detail with excruciating pain. That's not where the problem is. The problem is in the controller's head, with his need to control as much as possible and to have everything at his fingertips. It is impossible to do this, but he doesn't think so. He tries to control everything and may exhaust himself and waste his energy and talents. Once controllers accept your view that their system is failing, they will move to set the details right.

In order to insure an even flow of work, effort, and cooperation from these people it is necessary to maintain frequent contact with them, just as with the dependent (and for that matter most other) people. Nothing gets managed properly without frequent contact. Set deadlines. Discuss fresh ways of looking at the problem. Always keep the goal in view. While such people are often able to solve a given problem quite well, they may have difficulty isolating the most important problem out of a group.

Controlling people secretly suspect that they may be wrong. When you point out their mistakes, they will soon appear doubtful, sad, and amenable to suggestions. Again, never attack individual details; they will be difficult to refute. If they doubt the worth of their system and admit that the situation is out of control, they may abandon their rigid details themselves. But they will never abandon their system because you disprove a minor point.

When someone acts controlling under stress, manage him the same way. Redirect him in the direction you want.

The Competitive Type

These people seem aggressive, outgoing, always out to prove a point. On the surface, they are more able to get along with other people than the dependents and the controllers, and they are often admired and esteemed. In fact, that is their goal in life: to have others look up to them, respect them, or desire them, which is why they frequently put others down to place themselves in a better position. They hate to lose, and make obnoxious winners: *winning to them invariably means that someone else is losing*.

These people respond to stress with action. At the same time, they may seem a bit stereotyped or automatic in their response and a bit insincere. They may act like a salesman who is not really convinced of the value of the product he is selling; he's just convinced of the worth of making a sale.

In spite of their competitiveness they may not feel secure about themselves. They appear to be playing a role that they think they should like. They are so afraid of putting down the mask, looking in the mirror and deciding for themselves who they are, that they never really seem able to find the role that fits them best. They do not dare to be themselves, or try to discover who they are, because they might not come out as well as they wish.

Such people struggle to achieve recognition. They are looking for reassurance that they are estimable.

Episode 3: A competitive type and the boss (the italicized words are the tip-offs)

BOSS: Well, it's been only three days and you have the report already?

ANDY: Well, I had this *brilliant idea* that showed me where you're *wrong* in your thinking. *You've got to stop* the deal at once.

BOSS (*bristling*): What did you find?

ANDY: Well, *you shouldn't have* made the Harris deal or the trade with Lewis or purchased Gordon Packing. *You muffed it!*

Andy is off and running. He has not done his research thoroughly enough to warrant making most of his statements. He is acting impulsively and aggressively, trying to create a crisis and to show the boss up. Andy is interested in coming out on top, but he hasn't done his homework. What is worse, he is only going to make the boss feel defensive and angry.

These people need firm limits, but are easier to manage than the dependents and the controllers, even if they make the most noise. Their competitiveness is directed at trying to look better than whoever happens to be around.

ANDY: I found something else important *that you also* missed!

BOSS: Hold on! Hold on! One at a time!
(*An excellent point.*)

163

Look, Andy, you know you are one of *the most valuable, one of the brightest people I have here*. That's why I put you on that job in the first place.

(*Andy wants to hear this.*)

But *you see so much more than other people* that I think you get too excited.

(*He makes a criticism sound like a compliment.*)

Now, what is your suggestion and why?

ANDY: What do you mean?

BOSS: What should the company do now and why?

ANDY: Well, *I can tell you what was wrong with other deals.*

BOSS: That's great. I want to hear it. But first, what should we do?

(*Keeps Andy on the point, which is: what to do—not how bright Andy is and how stupid everyone else is. He shows esteem and understanding for Andy.*)

I put you on this project because I felt you were the only one who could solve it. I knew you'd find out a lot. I also knew that it would take you some time.

ANDY: I'm preparing my answer now . . .

BOSS: Great, I know it will be your usual excellent work when it's finally ready . . .

How to deal with a person like Andy? Immediately concede to him that he is estimable and does good work. This is the point he is trying to prove by creating such confusion in his environment. Andy is more comfortable when everyone else is confused because then he does not feel so exposed. His real self is somewhere behind the role he is playing; he tries to stay concealed. As a result, he does not confront himself and may not grow or be able to profit as much from experience as he should.

More than any other group, competitive people feel discomfort and guilt about those they have put down when they approach success. Indeed many chronic failures have this kind of personality.

By showing Andy that you believe he is worthwhile and good, you stop his attack. Now he doesn't have to put you down in order to pull himself up. *You* just pulled him up. Andy usually needs frank praise to feel good. When he feels bad about himself he may tear others down, and his favorite targets are people in authority. The trick is to leave it up to Andy to prove (by doing something constructive) that your faith in him is not mistaken and that he is worthwhile. Reassuring him of his worth only makes him feel that he is under more pressure to perform, to please, and to accomplish. He does love praise.

The dependents, the controllers, and the competitives all have different attitudes toward life.

The attitudes of dependent people are determined by the way they are given to, cared for, or loved. The controlling person's attitudes reflect how he feels about keeping intact and managing the "things" in his life in an orderly, predictable fashion (and of course he is greatly affected by how solidly in control he feels). The competitive person's attitudes are shaped by his fears of being retaliated against and by how well appreciated or esteemed he feels (which goes along with tearing others down).

People want to be reassured that they are the special person they want to be. For example, a controlling person likes to be told he is powerful, strong, solid, reliable, and predictable.

You can write your own ticket to success with anyone if you understand what he is, because then you know what he needs to be. You should not overstate your praise. Be genuine. Offer some concrete examples when you do laud him. It's not a matter of lying to him, but of taking the time to emphasize his good points. His reaction will be that you are an insightful, sensitive, understanding, intelligent, and reasonable person. And he will be right! He will also regard your opinion as reliable, and will say you are "like him" since you agree and define him so well.

Because he feels your judgment of him is so accurate there is every reason for him to assume that your judgment of other people is equally good. It is not very difficult to convince him that you know what you are talking about or to get him to take your word for what he does not know.

Don't Expect To Win If You're Rigid

When a person is a very rigid character type of any kind, his ability to win is limited to the extent of his rigidity. Unable to bend and compromise with others, he finds the world often opposed to him and is himself unable to change his fate. Winning depends on flexibility and resilience. While a rigid person may achieve limited goals, the price he pays is his lack of spontaneity and openness to himself and the people around him.

When a person becomes afraid, he becomes difficult to manage. It is not always possible to know exactly what is bothering someone, but by observing how they act you will find valuable clues to understanding them and to managing them. You already know something about the basic attitudes of the different character types and which situations they find most difficult. To manage anyone under stress, first determine whether he is acting helpless, competitive, or controlling and respond to him as if he were a character who typified that behavior.

When any person acts *helpless*, regardless of how he usually appears, he should be managed as the boss managed Rick. At the time a person feels helpless, he acts like a dependent person. If you reassure him of his worth, he will soon calm down. He needs to know what you still care.

When someone acts *controlling* under stress, he is probably afraid of losing control of himself. Manage him as you would a controlling character like Karl; keep him on the point by redirecting his efforts without debating his fine points.

Finally, when someone becomes *competitive* under stress, he is expressing a need for esteem, just like Andy. Using the same techniques, showing him that you admire him, will make him feel more comfortable, less threatened, and as a result less competitive.

If a person does not seem to fit any one of these types it is still possible to use these techniques to handle him. A person need not act helpless to deserve your reassurance. In fact, if you reassure someone early—when he feels most uncertain—you may prevent problems from arising later on.

You'll Save Time in the Long Run

It is possible to use these methods in everyday situations. You may believe that they are too time-consuming compared to the way you presently work. It's true: they may *be* more time consuming, but only initially. It takes time to observe others' behavior, to understand it, and to discuss it with them. Always begin these discussions with a comment about the other person's strong points and present them as if they were proof that he can and will do better. In an age as hurried and as impersonal as ours this is seldom done.

If you do take the time to follow these basic ideas, to listen and understand, the people you have to deal with will seem much more sympathetic to your cause, much more helpful, and less likely to get in the way. You will discover that you have saved time over-all by taking more time at the beginning because progress is smoother and people are grateful for your understanding. These methods are directed at helping you to help others do their best—not to pull the rug out from under them.

What use is it to allow your plans to be upset when people become rigid, act helpless, controlling, or compete with you? Helping people to attain a worthwhile goal, even if it is not their own, or keeping them from obstructing a worthwhile goal, is more valuable than allowing them to work in their old obstructive ways. By applying these principles for managing anyone who acts in these disruptive ways, you can remove others from your way, and win their esteem and good-will at the same time.

IF LIFE COULD go along smoothly and predictably the way you would like it to, trains would run on time, telephones would always work, people would be polite and mind their own business. But that's not the way life goes. Just when you have your mind set on a peaceful evening at a restaurant, the waiter decides he doesn't like your nose or ears and refuses to look in your direction.

Everyone is a pain in the neck sometimes, but some people seem to have a special knack for being disagreeable, for forcing themselves on others and being a nuisance, particularly some salesmen, taxi drivers, and waiters. There are ways of dealing with these intrusive people and coming out on top.

When these annoying people contradict themselves and make obvious errors, point them out; act as if by doing so you have won your point, and that there is no need to discuss the matter further. Again, if your goals are not served, you are just not interested in the other person's explanation, no matter what it is. Be firm—not argumentative. Know your rights and your limits. If they are violated, protest immediately, clearly, and directly. If you cannot get immediate satisfaction, don't wait! Go over the annoying person's head, stating your goals and limits to his supervisor. Don't be taken in. Speak up!

The Case of the Rude Phone Operator

One of the most common irritations is having to deal with a rude telephone operator. You can prevent problems from arising if you ask the operator for her number or name *before* you ask for her assistance. If the operator won't give you her number, hang up and try again. She's the type who will give you a problem later on. When the operator does give you her number, she knows that you can report her because you've literally "got her number." She has lost her anonymity. As soon as this happens, she is subject to the same fears of being exposed as anyone else. But sometimes you'll not remember to ask for her number. Here's a way out:

Speak to the Person in Charge

OPERATOR: Look, sister, I don't check out the lines. You'll just have to wait until tomorrow.

CALLER: That's absurd. I have to get through.

OPERATOR: That's tough, honey, but you can't get treated special around here. Nobody's special to the telephone company.

CALLER: Can I speak to your supervisor?

OPERATOR: What for? She won't be able to help you.

CALLER: Give me the supervisor.

Don't waste your energy with this woman. She'll only bring you trouble. Call the supervisor immediately and be firm and insistent. State how rude the operator was and how important the call is. That may not seem terribly helpful to you, but there is a lesson to be learned: *you just can't deal satisfactorily with people who can remain anonymous to you.* Know who they are as soon as you can and get them to reveal their identity, or else limit your exposure to them to the minimum or avoid them altogether.

The Loudmouth Taxi Driver

The world is full of other difficult people, like loud-mouthed taxi drivers:

You've got a prize headache that could have been run-ner-up in the last annual headache-of-the-year contest at King of Prussia, Pennsylvania. All you want is a taxi to go across town, quickly and quietly. The right strategy:

Don't Play for Sympathy

DRIVER: One goddam thing after another! You know what I mean. Look at that son-of-a-bitch cut me off (*honking*). Hey, you jerk! What do you think this is? Huh? What's the matter with you? Hey, you bum (*honks*)!!

PASSENGER: Driver, I would really appreciate it if you would be quiet. I've got a headache.

Terrific! But what do you suppose will happen? You were polite and kind to this loudmouth, who considers having a headache (the excuse which his wife gives for not having inter-course with him) no excuse at all. In his mind, you and his wife are in the same category: *fakers!* You know what you are going to get for your trouble? Don't guess: it's called an argument:

DRIVER: Oh, I'm sorry, mac. I didn't know you were so sensitive. I mean, look at you in a nice suit and big income. You don't have to drive with everyone cutting you off like I do (*slows down*). Maybe you'd prefer to walk.

RIDER: I really don't feel well. Please! Keep driving . . .

Wonderful! You are appealing to his humanitarian qual-ities, his sense of decency. But he's a loudmouth or worse. You *knew* that immediately. Why hope that he'll turn into a Red Cross nurse?

RIDER: . . . I really need some peace and quiet.

DRIVER: Look, mac! Why don't you go to the islands for a rest or take another cab? This here is a cab, not a sanitarium.

You waited fifteen minutes for this cab and you're very late. What should you have done, since you could tell he was a loudmouth at the beginning? You should have assumed absolute authority, adding a slightly menacing quality. Let's try it that way!

Act With Entitlement

DRIVER: Come on, you'd better hop in and . . .

RIDER (*cutting him off*): Driver, you'll take me to 67th and Madison.

DRIVER: Look at that son-of-a-bitch.

RIDER (*haughtily*): I do not believe I gave you permission to speak.

DRIVER (*stymied, and, boy, will he be*): *Wha?*

RIDER: Sixty-seventh and Madison! Do you have that?

DRIVER: Yes, and I . . .

RIDER: Very well, don't delay!

Your assumption is simply that it's his function to drive you in silence. Any time he is doing anything else, remind him of this obligation firmly and with total assurance. Just think of him as your paid chauffeur.

Here are a few other consumer-tested defenses against pests.

Sympathize-Empathize

There's another approach when you have a vexed driver who is angry at the world. Since you can tell he's angry as soon as you see him, sympathize with him. It makes you an ally, a friend. Remember, people who are angry have been hurt. A little sympathetic understanding works wonders.

172

RIDER: Sixty-seventh and Madison, driver.

DRIVER: Yeah. . . . Blah blah

RIDER: I can see you must be having a rough day. Everything gone wrong?

DRIVER: You bet. I think that . . .

RIDER: I've had days like that too. All you want is peace and quiet.

This can be very effective. I've seen it used successfully to convert obstinate, nasty cabbies into most willing and cooperative drivers.

Inhibit

Another solution is to be a bit psychopathic. You've got to be driven to the wall to use this one, but it works without fail. *Create a situation in which people are normally terrified of speaking.*

DRIVER: Blah Blah.

RIDER: Please! I just lost my mother this afternoon! I don't want any noise. I have to break the news. . . .

Sounds pretty manipulative and mendacious, doesn't it? Well, *you* know that you're reasonable, but that does not mean that the world is full of reasonable and good people or that you are going to be fully protected from the unreasonables everywhere you go. You have to have knowledge of at least some weapons to put the scales in balance. You probably would never use a statement like this. It's meant as an obvious example of an inhibiting situation. But if you are unable to deal with someone who is about to take advantage of you by using even less honest ploys on you, a person who cannot be reasoned with, inhibiting him may be a way to fight back.

173

Turn the Tables

Another psychopathic way to manage annoying people is to ask them for the very thing that they are asking you for. When the salesman knocks at the door, interrupt with a sales pitch of your own: try to sell him a cake. Ask for a favor. Try to borrow the taxi cab (or ten bucks) from a cabbie.

If you see a panhandler coming up to you on the street and you're waiting for someone and don't feel like walking to the next corner, what can you do? The guy reeks of liquor. Well, you can ignore him. You can call a cop. Most people won't, it's too upsetting and too unfair. Look at this down-and-out slob, who probably panhandles $8 to $10 per hour on this corner! He is pushing you very hard. Now he's following you. Now he's making nasty cracks and grabbing your sleeve. He looks seedy. Still, he makes you feel guilty just for being better off, which is the psychology of the panhandling profession.

BUM: How about that quarter, mac?
RESPECTABLE CITIZEN: Gee, let me look. Well, what do you know about that! I'm all out. God! My wallet's gone! Hey, did you take my wallet? Hey! Just a minute! Wait!

That should do it. Other statements you can try are: "Isn't this funny! I'm the one whose flat broke! Look, can *you* lend me a dime to call home?" You'll see him move off. If he doesn't at first, just persist. He will.

Be Unpredictable

Do the unexpected. Annoying people expect you to be defensive and passive. They think you'll let a lot go by without comment. Bellboys are skilled at wheedling tips by intimidation. They stare at your forehead and wait for you to move your hand into your pocket. They depend on your feeling uncomfortable and so they can pressure you into over-tipping.

Service costs. If you expect service, expect also to pay, and do so before the bellboy has a chance to work on you. It will cost you much less than if you let the bellboy get to you first.

BELLBOY (*depositing bags*): Will that be all, sir?

GUEST: Yes, thank you very much. You've been most helpful (*tipping him reasonably*). If I want anything else, I'll call.

You have taken the lead and shown appreciation, both by tipping and in words, which, believe it or not, still do count for something. By acting sure of yourself, you can get away with the tip you were planning. Also, dismiss the bellboy. When you act awkwardly, you only make the situation difficult for yourself.

Accept the rules of the game. Unless you have fragile materials in your case and want to carry them in your own hand, allow the bellboy to take them. Better yet, act as if you expect the bellboy to take them. If you know beforehand how much you are going to tip, you're not going to be taken. Make whatever demands you feel you want. In time the service and the level of your tip will find their own balance.

By acting unpredictably in a situation where someone is giving you a hard time you slow them down. If you are not acting as he expects you to, he needs time to reconsider what he is doing. That moment's delay is what you're looking for—an extra minute to get your thoughts straight so that you can deal with him.

The extreme example of this technique is to act a bit crazy. This always puts people off and makes them want to have as little to do with you as possible. Or . . .

Be Direct

When you have a waiter who won't pay attention to you, try the obvious. Ask the waiter, "Will you take my order?" Just be direct. Don't get angry. Be reasonable. Frequently the waiter will be embarrassed because he will have made an honest mistake. When you don't act simply and straightforwardly, *you'll* end up getting angry and being offensive. If the waiter wasn't sullen before, he will become so. If you really have difficulty with the waiter, go directly to the maitre d', state the problem, and do so with a quiet assurance that shows you could not possibly be wrong. Don't demand your rights, just assume them.

MAITRE D': Yes? Is everything all right, sir?

CUSTOMER: No. I can't understand this. The waiter assigned to our table hasn't served us.

MAITRE D': Ah, but that is impossible. René is one of our best waiters. For years he has worked here. You must be mistaken!

CUSTOMER: Ask him to speak with both of us.

MAITRE D': Now?

This is an excellent point because you will hear both sides of the situation. Be firm, quiet, dignified. Remember: *you're* right.

RENÉ: I have no idea what he is talking about.

MAITRE D: You see, sir?

CUSTOMER: Perhaps then he can take our order now.

It is very difficult for the waiter not to comply at this point. If nothing happens, it is best to leave. Usually people won't do this because of the late hour or having no other place to go, etc. But it sometimes shocks the maitre d' into action.

Play Their Game

There are other people whose irritating persistence is meant to wear you down. Insurance salesmen are like this. They actually believe they are doing you a favor. The best way to handle insurance salesmen is quite simple. Say, "No!" If that doesn't work, just remember what their dream is: the big, big sale.

When a salesman calls you repeatedly, it is possible to shut him off quickly and keep him from calling back by playing his game. For instance, you could tell him you are interested in a great deal of insurance and are accepting bids from different agents. After you have looked over everyone's offer, you plan to go with the lowest bidder. Say that you don't want to see anyone individually and will not even consider doing business with anyone who calls twice. You will call him if his program is the cheapest. And hang up. You have nothing more to say. You will get letters asking for follow-up visits. Forget them.

Just remember that *a simple "No" is where these people are trained to begin their pitch*. You have to play their game. Give them something to grab for, but make one of the conditions that they do not call you. Make it the first condition. If they don't like it and call you, just inform them that they have been removed from consideration and hang up. Don't argue! They're waiting for an opening. Let's see their sales managers get around this one!

Enlist Help

Being direct has its advantages. When someone cuts in front of you when you're standing in line, or takes your place, or is otherwise unfair to you, state clearly, *"You don't belong there! That is not your place!"* Then you can speak on behalf of everyone else in the line, "We've all been waiting our turn and we don't think you should walk in!" Turn and look to others. Encourage their disapproval of the intruder. He'll back off. People don't expect to be confronted like this. They assume no one will call them on their intrusion.

There isn't a reader who has not been taken advantage of, who has not backed down when he should have asserted his rights and authority because he feared making a scene or being disapproved of.

Remember: the intruder is probably as much afraid of making a scene as you are, and his plans depend on your compliance. If you act to assert your rights, he is flustered and put on the defensive.

To put someone on the defense when he is doing something wrong, ask simple direct questions or make simple statements:

1. "What are you doing?"
2. "Are you supposed to be doing this? Says who? Let's ask him!"
3. "This is not right!"
4. "No."

Then follow that by stating a simple fact:

1. "I was ahead of you."
2. "You still haven't done what you promised."
3. "It still does not work."
4. "No, that's final. I mean it! Do not discuss it further!"

Just stating the obvious in a simple way, without flooding the situation with needless anger, will make your point more effectively than anything else. It will put the other fellow on the spot very nicely. And what's best, it will get you off of the spot.

Again, *the person most likely to get you in trouble, is you.*

SALESMAN (*shows form on clipboard*): I'm conducting

a market survey to test how effective certain advertising is. May I come in to ask you some questions?

LADY OF THE HOUSE: I suppose.

Big mistake! She doesn't know what is going on. She's afraid to appear ignorant, so she's going to let this man in. Very stupid of you, lady, even if he doesn't turn out to be a burglar or a rapist.

SALESMAN: Have you ever seen the TV show "Pick a Million"? Very big nationwide show.

LADY: No.

SALESMAN: Or "Geraldine Faces the Facts"? or "Break-up"?

LADY: No.

SALESMAN: What about "Bonanza"?

LADY: Sure! I've seen that.

SALESMAN: Did you ever see a Whittier Reference set on TV?

LADY: No. . . .

A reference set means a set of encyclopedias. Many people like this lady are too afraid of appearing ignorant to ask what it means. So she never gets to hear the buzz word "encyclopedia," which would make her throw the guy out on his index. She just sits there and listens to him play to her ego. *Are* you ready?

SALESMAN: Ah, that's what we've been finding. I guess our advertising just hasn't reached the right people. We're trying to change from nationwide advertising to local advertising, to get local people to endorse our product. We'd be willing to pay them just like big sports stars get paid and print their picture in our newspaper with a letter from them. I know it'd be a bother for you to be given publicity, but we could use it and we'd pay.

The lady is given a set of encyclopedias "absolutely free." But to make the endorsement sound authentic, the company would like her to keep up the yearbook at her expense, $29.95 a year, so her neighbors will know she was sincere when they read her endorsement in the paper. Sound fair enough? Sure does—to *her*. So she takes the yearbook for ten years and it's a deal. It costs her about $300. Her kids never read the set and she'll wonder why the ad with her name never appeared; it almost never does!

The people who upset you the most are people who take advantage of your greed. You don't get anything for nothing. Ever! No matter what your Uncle Charlie told you. For nothing, you get nothing. The extent to which you believe the opposite is the extent to which you are a potential loser. If you have not come to grips with this fact, you're looking for the easy way out and that makes you very vulnerable. If you are waiting for your ship to come in and aren't at the helm of that vessel, you're going to wait one hell of a long time.

Don't rely on other people to help you out. You have to make it on your own. This doesn't mean that people won't give to their friends. They will, but not forever. Depending on other people to give you what you want is the surest way of being a loser because you never become independent . . . you never become free.

Here's Your Achilles Heel

The oldest game in the world is convincing someone that he is going to get something for nothing. You will be told that you are going to get rich quick, that you are going to become famous overnight, that you will have power and influence, and for all this you have to do practically nothing. Just stand naked in front of the mirror some Sunday morning, without holding your stomach in and without combing your hair or clearing your throat. Now say the following sentence to that serene, alluring image in the mirror:

"Is there any reason why others should not give me anything I desire?"

That's pretty dumb isn't it? Well, when someone takes advantage of you, it is probably because you expect them to give you something you neither deserved, had laid claims for, nor established your rights to. Each of us has a wish to be discovered as worthy, deserving, esteemed. Look, if you're so wonderful why hasn't someone done a lot more for you before? Why should someone want to *now*?

The housewife standing at the door imagines her picture in an ad in the local newspaper, telling why she bought the reference set and what she thought of it. She secretly believes that the man at the door knew that she was special, that by going along with him she would be recognized for being special. After all, the company wants *her* opinion, *her* letter, *her* picture and, lest we forget, her $300. Imagine! She actually believes the company values her intelligence and thinks that her neighbors would want to imitate her by buying their product.

Nobody ever cons anyone all by his own steam. You just cannot con another person without help. *People always con themselves*. Stop helping the con man! The con man finds out what others want and makes them think that this is what they are getting through him. The fact that the victims have to give a great deal is minimized or placed in a different light. The money for the yearbook is trivial compared to the glory and esteem you'll get. The con man says he sees in you the qualities that *you* yourself believe make you special, the qualities which no one else has seen up till now (good judgment, authoritative in your community, etc.). Like everyone else, you still feel insecure about your worth. When someone supports your hopes for yourself, you become vulnerable and may end up purchasing only their esteem, even though you may not realize this. If a buyer must beware of anyone, let him first beware of himself.

If the lady knew that nothing comes from nothing, the encyclopedia salesman's visit would have turned out quite differently. The proper strategy:

Ask Questions

Always ask questions when you are being pressured.
Con men rely on your unwillingness to expose your ignorance.
Down deep, almost everyone is pretty ignorant, so join the club.
Ask questions and don't be satisfied till you really understand. If
you can't understand—delay the decision until you do.

SALESMAN: I'm conducting a marketing survey of . . .
LADY: What's a marketing survey?
SALESMAN: To tell how well a product is being mar-
keted.
LADY: What product?

Great! Ask away! Interrupt the other guy's pitch as soon
as you have a question. If there is an answer that he would like
to postpone until later, it's probably because it's damaging to his
argument.

SALESMAN: We'll come to that in a minute.
LADY: What product are you talking about?
SALESMAN: A reference set. We've been on TV (*his
pitch is breaking up*).
LADY: What's a reference set?
SALESMAN: A reference collection.
LADY: I still don't know what you're talking about.
SALESMAN: Reference books.
LADY: For what purpose?
SALESMAN: For looking up facts of general knowledge.
LADY: Is that like an encyclopedia?
SALESMAN: Yes.
LADY: Good-bye!

A childless couple in their fifties was about to sign an
encyclopedia contract binding them to a purchase they would

never use. The salesman was brand new and embarrassed. His conscience just wouldn't let him go through with the deal when he saw how poorly the couple's house was furnished. He sensed there was something dishonest about the method, so he asked if they knew they were buying an encyclopedia. They said that they were only buying the annual supplements. He explained that the entire purchase would cost them over $300 and even came right out and asked whether they would buy the set, including the annual supplements, if they saw it in a bookstore at that price. They said they wouldn't.

"Then why are you buying it now?" he asked. The couple just shrugged. These people insisted that the salesman allow them to "have" the set of encyclopedias. Only when the salesman told them that he wouldn't even want their letter of endorsement did they throw him out of the house.

No, You're Not a Paragon

If you think you are so wonderful and powerful that your words should be chiseled on granite for all time, you are in trouble. If someone can make you believe he is aware of (and appreciates) your special qualities, he can rob you blind and you will stand up and thank him for it. You must become aware of this Achilles heel. Is it a need for praise and renown, a need to exercise control, or power—or success without struggle. Take a good look at yourself, ladies and gentlemen, because there is someone out there who will, in case you won't, and he'll manage to get to you every time. If someone else can figure out what you're really looking for, why can't you?

You can, and when you do, why not go out and get it by yourself, instead of waiting for someone to come around and offer it to you as tribute? People will believe and trust anyone who tells them what they want to hear and will defend him against all criticism.

Your worst Achilles heel is vanity, sucker!

To protect yourself, *ask questions everywhere and anytime*. This will disrupt other people more than anything else. Remember: they hope you'll obey meekly in order not to give away your ignorance.

If the emperor looks naked to you, say so! State the obvious and don't argue about it. Merely repeat it. Finally, don't let any of these disagreeable types *rush* you into anything. Rushing is their big ally. If you are moving faster than you want, you will be anxious and reach for anything that seems secure that these people offer you. And you can be sure that whatever you are offered under these pressured circumstances is not going to be to your advantage.

Practice saying: "Please slow down. . . . You're going too fast for me." You can only win at your own pace, not someone else's.

THE FIRST THING to know about winning with muggers and housebreakers is this: YOU CANNOT WIN WITH MUGGERS AND HOUSEBREAKERS—SO DON'T TRY. Read this over to yourself several times and believe it. So the object here is not winning; it is losing as little as possible.

When you are confronted by a mugger, assume that you are not going to be spared—not even cab fare home. Assume it, expect it, accept it. If you don't, you might end up dead. Assume that the attacker is desperate, anxious, impulsive, not terribly bright—and you'll be right almost every time!

Muggers come in several varieties, all unpleasant and all potentially dangerous. The first variety is the run-of-the-mill foot pad who finds that threatening people and robbing them is the easiest way of getting money. You have to be very stupid to be this kind of crook, since it involves an absolute minimum of planning. This type looks for someone who is alone on a poorly lighted street. These people do not even have the limited foresight to plan an effective robbery involving breaking and entering. They tend to be impulsive, unpredictable, and volatile.

Just Give In—and Fast!

Give them everything they want! You can begin by saying, "You can have everything I have, but please don't hurt me." Even tell them what you have on you. Say, "Here's all my money," and hand it over. If they ask for a watch or a ring just hand it over without a moment's hesitancy. You stand the best chance if the mugger feels you are easy, because then he'll relax. Accept the fact that you have already lost everything as soon as you are approached by the mugger. In spite of this, there is the possibility that you will be injured, but it is far less likely than if you are uncooperative.

Try to show as little anger and irritation as possible. Such feelings will only antagonize these people, and they may take their anger out on you. It is a good idea never to carry less than twenty or thirty dollars on you, so that a potential mugger will feel he has accomplished something by robbing you and no longer feels he has to beat you up in angry disappointment. Holdups in which a victim is murdered for a few dollars generally happen because the thugs got angry that they had taken a risk and received little in return.

Thugs think that way. When they steal, they take a risk. They may get caught. If they find no money they feel cheated because they took the risk for nothing. All of a sudden, they feel that they are the injured party! Since you are the only one around at the time, they may try to vent their anger on you. So do carry money for this eventuality. And stop being a smart guy about what "rights" you have. You don't have any rights. All you have is your life. Try to keep it.

The next kind of mugger is a young tough who is looking for money *and* for a fight. He is usually very frightened and tends to travel in a group. If you challenge him and make him even more afraid, he will try to show you how tough he is. This type overreacts to everything. Keep your big mouth shut with these raiders. Do what you're told, and quickly, or you are going to be injured way beyond your expectations. These people have a gripe to settle with authority and you may symbolically represent it. Whatever you say can be used to reinforce their prejudices and will work against you and quickly. They're *look-ing* for an excuse to hurt you.

The next type of mugger is an addict desperate for money. These people have very poor judgment. This is not to say that the others are sound thinkers, but that addicts have a special drive that thrusts them into action and out of control. They care even less for the consequences of their act than the other types. Just give them what they want and let them run away.

How Good Is Self-Defense?

If you are alone when you are being mugged, and no one else is in the vicinity, don't get smart and blow a police whistle or battery-operated siren. You'll get creamed. The only time that's right for sounding an alarm is when there are people nearby who can *immediately* assist you. If there are not, just be polite, quiet, and deliberate in your moves, and give the muggers what they want.

If you have trained in karate or in any other form of self-defense you should abandon any intention of using your training. There are exceptional occasions, I suppose, but they are few. Perhaps if you were attacked on the beach by someone your size and you could tell that he wasn't armed, you might consider using your skills to defend yourself. Otherwise, forget it. Even if you have trained very hard for a few years, one good thrust with a knife is going to slow you down and the next thrust will follow close behind. Karate is a sport. Mugging is not. Maybe your instructor could come out on top. Why don't you just be cooperative, give the mugger all your money and discuss what your instructor would have done to the mugger at your next lesson?

When you think you're *about* to be mugged, move toward a street light or toward the nearest thoroughfare, toward the largest concentration of people. That is often enough to discourage the mugger. If it isn't and the suspicious person is still approaching, you could yell. He might panic and run away, but he might also try to get closer to silence you. Remember: if you are alone, assume you've lost everything. Your object is to survive. If you come out of the situation unharmed, you are a winner.

The Burglar's Psychology Is Different

A burglar who breaks into your house is likely to be a different kind of person. He's much less interested in doing you physical harm. He just wants your valuables, and he wants to get out of there as quickly as possible.

Never corner a burglar! This will make him panic and attack. Don't block the exit. Give him room to escape. It's not your job to catch him. Don't pick up a gun and have a shoot-out. You are most likely to kill one of your own family, maybe someone looking to see where his birthday presents are hidden. If you are upstairs, and the burglar is downstairs, you can make noise to frighten him away. But don't confront him. Call the police, make a commotion, and you'll hear him go. Confront him and he'll do anything to get out of there, including killing you.

Burglars call their breaks "jobs," which gives you an idea of how they see their work: less impulsive and more regular than mugging.

Everyone has heard stories of someone who has foiled a burglar or a mugger. *Don't be taken in by these tales.* They are almost always exaggerated to make the teller appear to be a bigger hero than he really is. Enjoy the story for what it is—a story. The only incidents in which a robber is foiled and the would-be victim's actions might be called prudent involve a robber who is unarmed, much smaller, intoxicated, confused, or overdosed with drugs; in other words, when the act of foiling the crime was a push-over, not really heroic, and not worth telling about. But if you change the details a little, it sounds great and really impresses your secretary and friends.

The best way to handle all these people is to avoid places where muggers are likely to be and to make your home uninviting to burglars.

19 / HOW TO WIN AT WHEELING AND DEALING

ANYBODY WHO says his book can teach you how to bargain and haggle isn't telling you the truth. You learn to wheel and deal by wheeling and dealing, and to master these techniques you are going to have to pay a price. After a few experiences—bargaining for a car, arguing over the cost of painting their home, or working out a repair job with their local service station—people learn a great deal and pay for it. Think of this chapter as a scholarship to help lower your tuition in the school of negotiating.

Before negotiating, you must make some decisions. First, determine what and how much you would like to receive as the result of the negotiation—what you would consider an acceptable solution. This should be what you would be *happy* to receive, not the *most* you could receive—just what would make you *reasonably* happy, be it money, privileges, or rights. If you don't know what will make you happy before you begin, you may pass up a chance to close a deal that may not come again.

Next, determine the high and low points that make up the range of what you will accept, just so you know where you stand while you're negotiating.

Finally, pick a point below which you absolutely refuse to negotiate. This is the *walk-away point*.

Now try to figure out what the other side has set for *its* goals.

Confusing? Perhaps, but not so confusing as the situation will be if you fail to determine these guidelines beforehand.

How To Sell a House for Top Money

One situation in which these techniques are especially helpful is buying and selling a house. Here are the steps to implement this method. (Assume that you're the seller in the following example; the principles apply to the buyer, too, but in reverse.)

1. *Determine the actual market value of the house* according to the best possible estimates. If in doubt, call in an appraiser. Let's suppose he says your house is worth $50,000 in today's market. Let's assume you paid $30,000 for the house years ago and have made $10,000 worth of improvements. You would like to make some profit, about $10,000.

2. *Establish a target price of the house*: $48,500 to $52,500. This is the price you would be pleased to receive for your property.

3. *Establish the lowest price you would consider*: $40,000 plus selling expenses plus a small profit—$43,000.

4. *Establish the other person's range in your own mind.* Chances are he would like to buy the house for $40,000 and probably would not pay over $50,000.

5. *Determine your asking price* by adding 10 to 15 percent to the market value. So you will ask $55,000 to $57,000.

6. *Open with the asking price* and do not move away from it until a counter-offer is made by the buyer. To make a deal you must know whether he's serious and within your range. When the counter-offer is made, do *not* respond to it. Do continue to discuss the values of the house. It is very important for you to withhold any mention of at least some improvements and features of the house so you can reveal them at a later stage of the inevitable haggling. Reveal only one such improvement at a time and discuss it in great detail. Act as if you did not hear the counter-

offer. When you are finished describing an improvement lovingly, then is the time to direct your attention to the offer.

BUYER: I don't think you heard me; I offered you $40,000 for the house.

SELLER: I didn't think you were being serious. If you'd like to make a reasonable offer, I'd be pleased to consider it.

Do not budge one inch until the buyer offers a price above the walk-out point, in your case $43,000. It's not worth your energy to talk further unless he's going to bid above this amount. If he's not, you've already decided beforehand that you won't do business with him, anyway. If you come down in response to an unreasonable offer (and $40,000 would be stealing your house) you would only reward the buyer for being unreasonable, You want to reward him only for being reasonable, right? You should know that by now!

There's a Time To Stall

When the buyer finally does come up to your base-line price, stall for more time. You should do something now to shift the tone of the negotiations. Perhaps your wife could discuss some of the improvements she has made. This tactic is called "changing the negotiator" and is effective for putting the other party off guard. Such a switch is very useful in any kind of negotiation; just when the other party thinks he has figured you out, he is presented with someone else to figure out.

Let your wife talk about the rugs that you're including in the deal, the plantings, anything at all. It may be interpreted as only chatter and may be a little bit annoying to the buyer. But that's all right even if it doesn't make complete sense. You want him to become a little bit annoyed and you want him to become a little bit anxious. He should be made to think that he has a good bargain going and should be afraid of losing it.

Another way of managing this tactic is to defer to your wife by asking what she thinks and have her briefed in advance to give no immediate answer. The buyer will wait for her response, but when she does finally speak, it is to give more selling points about the house. Irritating, but it usually makes the buyer try to close.

It is a good idea to ask the buyer how he has gone about evaluating the worth of your house and then to disparage his methods of determining the price as unrealistic. Does he know the cost of labor, supplies, etc? The idea is to make the buyer feel that his methods of determining the price are faulty, that he cannot rely upon them. It's a good tactic to get the other side to question its judgment!

SELLER: I imagine you must have set some value for this house.

BUYER: Sure, I think it's in the low forties somewhere.

SELLER: Do you have any idea how much this kitchen cost?

BUYER: Sure! Around $3,000.

SELLER: Maybe ten years ago! The kitchen cost $4,500 and that was two years ago! Your figures are old. Really, you don't know how much this house is worth! Much too low!

BUYER: Well, what do *you* think the true worth is?

Caution: don't give an exact answer or one that destroys your position. Mention the top of your acceptable range as your first idea of a compromise—$52,500. This makes you appear to have come down in price. The buyer has come up to $43,000. The midway point between the two prices $52,500 and $43,000 is about $48,000—right where you want it to be. Right now you are in a position of trying to move down as much as he will move up in order to get to your target.

Each time you move in price you should give the impression that your offer is final. When you are very near what you want, it could be useful to have your wife indicate that she felt the last offer was too low and that she would not consider it. See if this forces the buyer up. If it doesn't, ignore your wife's comment. It was only a tactic anyway.

It's Time for a Private Huddle

It is sometimes useful to call for a private huddle with your wife (or a business associate) at a critical time to create pressure toward an agreement or to make a dramatic offer. The point of calling a conference is merely to upset the pace of the negotiations. You already know where the discussion is going; all you want to do is create more anxiety in the buyer's mind to speed the process up.

SELLER: Well, we've talked it over and we can't accept $45,000. The house is worth much more than that, and $48,000 is as low as I can go.

If the buyer wants to think it over, make some arrangement for him to call you; *do not call him*. Whoever calls first is somewhat at a disadvantage.

When you have reached the price range you believe reasonable, it is considered part of the game of negotiating to continue to bring out further assets or other points that you feel the buyer has missed. This will give you time to see how much farther you can go. When you are fairly sure you can do no better—and you're at that point where you had decided you could be happy—close the deal!

It is useful during negotiations to appear a bit deaf occasionally. It is also useful from time to time to appear to be on the brink of acting irrationally. Surprisingly enough, the other side may act to prevent upsetting a negotiator who looks as if he is going crazy. This is a beautiful negotiating tactic when it works and if the negotiator does not remain crazy for too long. Remember: most people are very afraid of upsetting others and try to avoid doing so.

You Can't Avoid Risks

Negotiating is a game. The object is for your side to make the other side feel that they will miss a great opportunity if they don't accept your terms. A negotiator must be willing to risk losing everything in order to win. It may seem contrived and artificial to people who do not regularly negotiate to act this way when they are selling property, but it is better to become involved in an artificial negotiation than to sell your hard-earned possessions too cheaply. During a negotiation accept the following statements:

It's a game. The other side is "the enemy." You are adversaries. You don't want to be their friend. They don't want to be your friend. You want to buy or sell at the price you want. Anything else is irrelevant. Later you can have a drink on it. Finally you should never get angry during a negotiation about anything that is reasonable from the other party's point of view, such as a low bid. Just see the bid as a ploy, a tactic, and counter it. The *purpose* of the low bid may have been just to get you angry.

And don't forget to use the other skills that were discussed before, especially how to listen and how to argue.

Everyone has a price he is willing to pay for what he wants. The currency can be time, money, discomfort, position, or love. You should know what you're willing to give up. While you may not use all the methods discussed here, understanding them allows you to observe what is going on in your opponent's mind as he yields and struggles with you—and also to recognize his ploys.

Winning often depends on understanding the tactics and the politics of negotiation. You don't want to walk out too soon. You don't want to stay too late. You just want to win. And you can!

IN MARRIAGE, if both of you don't win, both of you lose.

Winning in marriage seems more difficult than in any other relationship because the parties are so close. As I have shown, making the right decision requires the talent to see events clearly and in perspective. But when two people are involved in marital difficulties, so many emotions become uncorked that their vision becomes cloudy. The objectivity of the participants is often the first casualty of a marital battle. Distortions are accepted as facts, jealousies become realities, momentary grudges are mistaken for long-standing attitudes, and innocent habits are interpreted as personal attacks.

It becomes a mess.

It's easier to tell why marriages go wrong than why they turn out well. Many marriages fail because the rights to privacy, trust, and the benefit of the doubt are not respected.

FRED: Susan, Where are you? . . . Susan? (*storms around the house, looking in the cellar, the kitchen . . . finally finds a note on his dresser . . . reads:*)

"Dear Fred, I will be home late. I've set a place for you. Just heat up what's on the stove, and try not to make your usual mess. Susan."

Fred is beside himself. Susan sometimes meets one of her friends in town and has dinner with her after going shopping. It's not really a ritual; it's just something she does now and then. This time, Fred cannot stand it and boils over. When Susan does come home at nine o'clock he is ready to go ten rounds.

SUSAN: Hi, did you find my note?

FRED: Where the hell have you been? Do you know what time it is? What've you been up to?

SUSAN: Hey, wait a minute! Are we going through this routine again?

FRED: You bet we're going through this routine! You could have told me beforehand you were going out.

SUSAN: Every time I do you make a big stink about it and try to make me feel guilty about going out shopping with Anne. You'd think I was . . .

FRED: Go ahead, finish the sentence! "You'd think I was" *what*?

SUSAN: Messing around! Isn't that what you worry about?

FRED: What kind of a mouth have you got? What are you doing, trying to make me into some kind of madman? You're going to go too far! You have no right to go somewhere without telling your husband where you're going.

SUSAN: Where'd you read that—in some old marriage manual?

FRED: I absolutely will not put up with your running around all over town!

SUSAN: Running around? What do you call running around?

FRED: Don't act so cute, you . . . I know all about ladies in cocktail lounges.

SUSAN: Tell me about them, Fred! Tell me about all the ladies you know in cocktail lounges!

FRED: Stop trying to change the subject! Where'd you spend the afternoon?

SUSAN: In Bonwit's and in Saks.

FRED: What is that supposed to mean?

SUSAN: I don't know, maybe that I spent the afternoon in Bonwit's and in Saks.

FRED (*looking around*): Okay, let's see what you bought. I don't see any packages.

SUSAN (*irritated*): Oh, I must have left the packages at his apartment.

FRED: Don't you get funny with me!

SUSAN: Look, just cut this all out! Anne and I went shopping, had dinner at *Le Mistral*, and went home.

FRED: What time did you have dinner?

SUSAN: I refuse to answer any more questions. And do you know what, mister? I just refuse to talk about this situation any more.

FRED: I want to know what you were doing!

SUSAN (*starts cleaning up his mess in the kitchen*): You don't have any right to know what I was doing! I'm entitled to privacy and to have a world of my own and secrets of my own and not to feel I have to report to you every minute of the day what I'm doing.

FRED: Liberated woman! Oh boy!

SUSAN: Look, do you tell me everything you do?

FRED: That's different; you're not interested.

SUSAN: Get that, folks? That's a classic! I'm not interested because I don't go around prying into your affairs.

FRED: If you were interested, you'd be home to meet me after work.

SUSAN: I don't believe this! That's the same argument you used to give for why I couldn't get a job, because I wouldn't be home after school for the children. Because they'd get lonely and need a mother at home. Tell me, what do teen-age kids need a mother at home for after school? To be a witness to their fighting?

FRED: Boy, I just don't know what's happened to you! You think you can go any damn place you want! Doing God knows what and with whom!

SUSAN: All right, enough! You're getting crazy! (*puts the dish towel on his shoulder.*)

FRED: It's not enough! What about your other evenings out on the town?

SUSAN: What are you talking about?

FRED: Tuesdays. Take your goddamn towel! (*throws it.*)

SUSAN: You object to my taking a couple of courses at the adult education center? What's wrong with that?

FRED: Nothing's wrong with that. Oh, nothing, nothing at all.

SUSAN: You just can't stand not knowing what I'm doing every minute of the day! Well, you have a problem, because I'm not going to tell you. I'm not doing anything wrong, and I don't have to go through life hiding in the bathroom around here whenever I need privacy. I'm a grown woman and I have a mind of my own. Just because I find a few interests outside of this home doesn't mean that I don't care.

FRED: What's the matter with our marriage? Why isn't it satisfying you?

SUSAN: I keep on telling you: I need to do some things for myself—and by myself.

FRED: Like what . . . like the things you do these nights?

SUSAN: All right, Fred, I'll confess . . . I'm a prostitute and I split my time between the Hilton and the Americana. But don't worry: I use my maiden name. Jesus! (*makes a kerchief with the towel, puts it on her head.*) I'm very discreet.

Here's another couple where the shoe is on the other sex.

WIFE: You're going skiing!

HUSBAND: That's right. I told you last week that if there

was snow on the ground, I'd be going up to Vermont with Vic. A foot of new powder. Wow!

WIFE: You could have asked me along.

HUSBAND: You said you didn't want to go.

WIFE: That's because I could tell you really didn't want me to. You have more fun alone. I know, I can tell. (*Getting angry*) I know you prefer to be up there with Vic.

HUSBAND: I do like skiing with you—but with you being just a beginner it's kind of dull for me to take those easy slopes. It's okay some of the time.

WIFE: If I was a twenty-two-year-old blonde thing learning how to ski you wouldn't say that.

HUSBAND: That's beside the point. I like to ski expert trails and I don't like worrying about you falling every minute.

WIFE: You've taken all these lessons and you're so good it's almost like you got better to get away from me.

HUSBAND: That's the craziest reasoning I've ever heard in my life! I love skiing! I look forward to skiing all year. I love getting out on the slopes and really going at it.

WIFE: And you love meeting all the young girls in the bars and taking them back to your room!

HUSBAND: Look, I can't stop you from thinking whatever you want. But you must understand something. Skiing is more than something I *want*. It's something I *need*. Something that makes me more of a human being. It revitalizes me!

WIFE: I don't see why you can't get what you need from being with me.

HUSBAND: I get a great deal from you.

WIFE (*taunting*): But it isn't enough.

HUSBAND: No, it isn't. How about that?!

WIFE (*screaming, crying, and starting a real scene*): I knew it! You don't want me around! You want to go running all the time to these places. You don't have to go away all the time and stay overnight.

HUSBAND: You're being ridiculous! I go away only for

one night. I can't help it if the best skiing happens to be a five-hour drive from here. To drive ten hours in one day is crazy. . . . Look, if I wanted to fool around I could fool around in the daytime. I don't need the added expense of a motel room. You keep telling me you really don't like skiing. If I just want to be with you, I'd rather be doing something that both of us like. Skiing just isn't a good way of getting together.

WIFE (*crying*): You shouldn't go away. I have a right for you to be home. I have a right as a wife and mother to know that you're around, not running all over the place.

HUSBAND: Just because we're married, does *not* mean you have a right to take part in everything in my life. I have some rights, too! You don't fit into my plans all the time, but that doesn't mean I don't care about you.

WIFE: You tell me what it means.

HUSBAND: It means that sometimes it's very good to get away and be alone. I didn't sign a contract to spend every minute of the rest of my life with you. I go away to ski, not to fool around. The way you go at me every time I leave only gets me angry and makes it more difficult for me to enjoy myself. Why can't I ever leave for skiing with you telling me to have a good time and to enjoy myself? What's wrong with that? You always look at this as if I'm planning to hurt you.

WIFE: You do hurt me when you go away like this!

HUSBAND: I'm sorry about that, I really am, but I can't go around being your sole reason for living. It's too much of a burden on me. When you go out to play cards with the girls at night I don't give you the third-degree. Would you want me to come along and play with you?

WIFE: That's different. You don't play well and besides I've been Cheryl's partner for years. And *I* don't stay overnight when I play cards.

HUSBAND: It's the same thing.

WIFE: It's not. You just want to be away from me!

HUSBAND: Is there anything wrong with being away

from each other for a little while? Don't you think it's an opportunity to get a new perspective? It would be if you didn't land on me all the time, accusing me. You know, when you accuse me like that you belittle how much I feel about you and make me feel as if you don't believe I care.

WIFE: If you cared, you'd stay home!

HUSBAND: According to the way *you* feel. You've made some rules and you interpret them without giving one good goddamn what I feel. All you care about is your side of the argument. You've trapped yourself in a little world and you refuse to move out of it. You want everything to stay the same. We've known each other fifteen years. You've done absolutely nothing with yourself in those years to grow, and you expect me to stay the same, too. You've made me the central point of your life. It's not my responsibility to make you happy and content with yourself twenty-four hours a day. It wouldn't hurt *you* to go away with one of your girl friends for a few days and see what it's like being by yourself. It might do you a world of good.

WIFE: I can tell you want to get rid of me.

HUSBAND: No, I don't, but if you don't start giving me a little room to breathe you may end up pushing me out. If I stopped skiing and stayed home, all I'd do would be to resent you.

WIFE: What do you do now?

HUSBAND: If I resent you it's only because you make me.

WIFE: What about fooling around?

HUSBAND: If I did, it would be an accident and would be a physical thing. It would have nothing to do with our relationship.

WIFE: I just don't want any accidents to happen.

HUSBAND: There's nothing in the world you can do to prevent it if it's going to happen. And it can happen anywhere.

It can happen to you. My God, look at all the free time you have that I don't know anything about!

WIFE: Don't be ridiculous! I have no intention of fooling around. Don't be silly! Who would I fool around with?

HUSBAND: If you want me to accept that, you have to begin by accepting my story.

WIFE: That's different.

HUSBAND: As long as you believe that and push me, you're going to have trouble and you may end up making me do something out of spite.

Short periods away from each other have a beneficial effect on most marriage partners. These breathing spells offer a new perspective and a chance for each partner to clear his/her head. One summer in Balestrand, Norway, I met a woman from Bergen celebrating her fiftieth birthday. She had come to that small village for two weeks every summer since she had been married. She found it a source of constant enjoyment to be alone, to talk to whomever she wished, to eat when she wanted, to walk where she chose, or to stay in bed. For her, it was a time of thinking of herself first and taking stock of what she had done that year. The best part of being away, she said, was the sense of newness she felt and losing the feeling of being trapped. There's a lot to be learned by her example.

When partners do not trust each other or don't give each other the benefit of the doubt, the marriage almost inevitably becomes the kind of burlesque I've described in the two preceding arguments. Each party in a marriage is entitled to privacy and to a world of his own, and to develop a circle of friends and interests that keep him vital and alive. Sharing everything with one's spouse is not really possible anyway. *Two people cannot satisfy all of each other's needs all of the time*. To attempt to do so is only going to lead to more disappointments. When a spouse tries to force himself to like what the other is doing, especially when he really would like to be doing something else, it often leads to feelings that seem insincere. It would be much better in that case for each partner to share his or her special interest with friends who feel the same way. This reinforces the marital interest, is very supportive, and neither spouse feels resentful.

Something New Has Been Added

When two people allow each other to pursue individual interests independently of each other, they provide themselves with an opportunity to grow and to become more complete. Developing an outside interest can only turn each partner into more of a person, and that can have only good effects on the marriage because *each becomes more of a person to love and to be loved by*. In the time they do spend together they do what they both like; neither secretly feels that the other has been holding him back.

When each has an individual interest he also brings something new into the marriage—something new to talk about and share—and the relationship is rejuvenated. Each does not depend so intensely upon the other for support and reassurance, because each has found something in the world to make him feel secure as an individual. They are both able to give much more in such a marriage and are less likely to insist that the other be the sole source of emotional supplies.

It is the very nature of man that he is multi-faceted. In a marriage two people hopefully share many facets of their personality and life together, but it is utopian and self-defeating to expect that each partner will share all the interests and needs of the other, or that he will be able to fulfill them. Just because people get married does not mean that they no longer need other people. To deny this right is to inhibit the growth of you and your partner, to limit him to a restricted role, and to resist change. Resentment is sure to follow, and even simple needs which the partners could easily fulfill may then be left unmet.

If you aren't willing to give your partner privacy, trust, and the benefit of the doubt, there is really very little that you can give in other ways that will make up for it. How can you compensate for taking away the opportunity for growth? While it is not possible in many marriages for growth to proceed as it might have if the two partners had remained single, it is important to allow as much growth as possible, even if one partner does not feel entirely comfortable doing so.

There are other reasons why winning in marriage seems so difficult. Many marriages are built on a shaky foundation; the partners married the wrong person for the wrong reason at the wrong time. One cannot correct these mistakes merely by light-heartedly setting new goals, especially later on in a marriage when kids and financial obligations are involved.

When people marry before they have an opportunity to explore the world and to see what it has to offer them, they miss a great deal. They give up some of their freedom to grow, to discover, to choose. They often begin to think in terms of what is best for their marriage before they have had the chance to learn what is best for themselves as individuals. When decisions are made too soon in a person's life, before he knows what he wants, he may be compromising more than he realizes.

There is plenty of time to get married. Some people, of course, take years to make up their minds, and this statement does not apply to them. If you're not sure who you are or what you want to do with your life, you probably should not get married. You should have goals for your own life and be able to compare them with your intended spouse's to see if they conflict. If you don't bring the conflict out into the open, time will. The following case may seem extreme, but it illustrates the pitfalls of ignoring this advice.

Victor and Carol Married Too Soon

When Victor and Carol married they were both twenty-one. Neither had dated much before they began seeing each other. Victor's father had always criticized him for the slightest mistake. As a result, Victor was timid and afraid to try hard at anything he did. His self-confidence was always very low.

Carol was seventy-five-pounds overweight when they married, and that was after losing twenty-five pounds just to get into her wedding gown. She was thankful that someone was interested in marrying her. Besides, she made Victor feel secure; no one was about to carry her off. No one could lift her, to begin with.

After his father died, Victor began to be more aggressive and took over the family business. His self-confidence grew. In fact, he became a very good businessman, perhaps even better than his father. He was now free to become himself. Carol became terrified of the change in him and decided to go on a crash diet. After a while, Victor settled down and was content with his achievements, but a remarkable thing began to happen to Carol. Suddenly, at the age of twenty-seven, she began to bloom. She worked out at a gym and lost all her excess weight. The bulging, middle-aged housewife became a slender, very beautiful young woman. She looked much better than any girl Victor had ever even thought of dating. Wherever they went, she was complimented, and now Victor began to feel threatened.

Carol was thinking about herself in a new light. She realized that she had married Victor for security and out of fear that he was the only one who would ever ask her. Now she had a new self-image, and it was terrifying to Victor. Because she no longer felt insecure, she wanted to go out and meet people instead of staying home. In spite of the security that Victor had provided, he had not provided for her needs as a person, and she had never before emerged as a person. She had been only a terrified child. When Carol grew up, Victor found himself married to somebody new.

Victor wants the old relationship back, the nice, safe, and easy relationship. That's what he says. Actually, he wants Carol to be a little more presentable than she was before, but what is going on now just doesn't make sense to him. He's anxious and jealous all the time and Carol feels trapped.

What To Do When Both Partners Change

When people change their marital roles they are often unwilling to return to former attitudes. They have to look at themselves anew. It is true that Carol has changed. But Victor has, too. He is not the timid soul of yesteryear. And he needs to have the opportunity to believe that he can handle this newly blossomed woman. After all, it was only under his protection that she felt secure enough to grow. That's a point in his favor. He must discover his new worth and learn to believe in it. Once Victor admits that he has grown and that he also would not return to his former condition, it will be easier for him to tolerate Carol's growth. Who knows? If he can learn to see her progress as proof of his worth and strength, he may even begin to take pride in it.

Because early marriage makes self-discovery more difficult, it should be avoided until you are more certain of what you want. It is far simpler to determine your real goals and attitudes when there is only yourself to think about than when you have a family to consider. While married people often reach a new self-awareness at thirty or thirty-five, unmarried people may do so earlier. Marriages are usually more successful when the partners are older. *The best way to win is to wait.*

There is a way for you and your spouse to begin to look at your marriage together and to help each other redefine the goals in your marriage and make it work. The very first step is for you to sit down and talk about your life.

Are you happy doing what you are doing? Is there

something that you would like better? Are you content? Need help?

The following "Marriage Inventory" may be useful. But first be certain that you and your spouse both want to follow it through. Forcing someone won't work and may do harm.

A Marriage Inventory

Make a list of all the good points about your spouse—the traits you really feel are important, that you really love. Then list all the bad points.

Now make a list of what you believe are your goals for yourself. Then do the same for what you think your spouse's goals are for himself.

Ask your spouse to make a similar set of lists.

Don't discuss the lists for about a week. Just go over them several times and make certain that you really believe what you have put down.

Do not show your list to your spouse. The first time he/she should know what is on your lists is at a planned discussion.

Here are some sample lists (prepared by one couple who are having a considerable number of problems). These lists are to guide you. Subsequent comments will show what they reveal.

INVENTORY OF SPOUSE'S GOOD POINTS

HUSBAND'S LIST	WIFE'S LIST
good cook	hard worker
keeps house clean	good father
gets meals on time, usually	helpful around the house
never gets angry	helps with the kids
good with the children	tries to be affectionate

INVENTORY OF SPOUSE'S BAD POINTS

HUSBAND'S LIST	WIFE'S LIST
seems moody and sad a lot	sometimes is impatient
has a low sex drive	doesn't give me a chance to talk
doesn't like to argue	has to be right all the time
is tired a lot	wants sex whether or not I do
complains too much	doesn't take me seriously
too attached to her mother	thinks I'm superwoman
doesn't seem to appreciate me	almost certain he fools around
	watches TV too much

INVENTORY OF GOALS

HUSBAND'S LIST OF HIS OWN GOALS	WIFE'S LIST OF WHAT SHE THINKS HER HUSBAND'S GOALS ARE
better job	better job
more money	more money
better life for the kids	more sex
a big house	to get along better with me
time to go fishing	to spend more time with me
a satisfying sex life	to make a happy home for the kids

This woman is going to be surprised to find how far wrong she is. The husband is very self-centered and is really interested in his own pleasure. If he had more time and money he would probably spend less time with her.

HUSBAND'S LIST OF WHAT HE THINKS HIS WIFE'S GOALS ARE	WIFE'S LIST OF HER OWN GOALS
to improve sexually	to please him
to be more cheerful	to feel decent more of the time
to break away from her mother	to have more material things
to learn to complain less	to have a happy home
to be more appreciative	to spend more time together

This husband will also be surprised. In this list, not one of his items is related to her list. He does not see her as a person in her own right. He sees her as someone whose main purpose is to please him. If she is not pleasing him, then it is unimportant to him what she is feeling. His desires seem to crowd hers right out of his mind, and the only way he can see her is in terms of what he needs, not in terms of what she may want.

How to Use the Inventory

The next step after you've made your lists is to get a sitter for the kids and make reservations for a weekend somewhere where you will not meet anyone you know and where there is very little to do. The beach, off season, is a good place. So are mountain resorts, off season. If you are in the city, get out of it. Don't turn on the television, not even for the news. And don't make an elaborate production out of meals.

Sit down quietly in your room. Each of you should go through his first list, item by item, discussing each point until you have said everything you feel about it. Be sure you start with the first list. It is the easiest to work with, and it establishes points of agreement. Do not go on to the next list until both of you have completely talked out everything. Ask each other questions to fill out any points you are not sure about.

Move on to the next pair of lists in the same way, giving each other an opportunity to present your views without being interrupted. It should take several hours to go through the four pairs of lists together. Do not try to rush or to do them all at once. But if you do try to do them the same day, then spend the rest of that day discussing what each of you learned, feel, agree and disagree with. The next day after breakfast, separate for a few hours and, without referring to the old lists, make a new set of lists along the same lines as before. Then repeat the same process that day.

You should discover a great deal. No matter what happens, you will come away from this experience with a new perception of your spouse, yourself, and your marriage. Do you really know what's going on in your spouse's mind? What he feels, what he wants, what he thinks you want? You have a very enlightening experience in store for you.

Some points should not be brought up because they do not really help. Openly accusing the other partner of having an affair is not helpful. Generally, the only time an affair should be brought into the discussion is when the matter is obvious. If it is, then the involved partner probably was careless about it and such carelessness is often prompted by a wish to reveal it. Even then it's not always wise to discuss this emotion-charged issue because affairs are often only symptoms of other marital difficulties which the inventory should have flushed out for airing.

If you're aware of points that invariably create a storm you can talk about them, but save them for later, after the discussion is well under way, so that you do not sabotage the entire project.

You should state how you feel without going into great detail. "I still think your father did a rotten thing to you by giving the house to your brother" is enough. Your husband has heard your complaint many times before and already knows the details. And why are you bringing it up now? What is the point you wish to prove? That you think your husband is a jerk for not knowing better, or that his brother is a thief? Or do you just want to get some angry feelings off your chest? This kind of tactic is not useful. It only acts as a wedge keeping you apart. That's not what this is about.

All You Have To Lose Is Discomfort

It is difficult for either of you to win in your marriage unless each of you knows and shares the other's wishes and dreams and unless you have respect for each other's needs. This takes time, considerable effort, and sometimes discomfort. If you have not reconciled your differences until now, you probably already have plenty of the discomfort. And that's all you can lose by trying. Bringing out conflicting ideas will not make the problem worse; you are already in conflict. It's time for a resolution of problems even if it leads to an argument. Unlike winning other kinds of arguments, in a marriage each partner must make the other aware of his needs *beforehand*. Don't try to "psych" out your spouse or figure out how to take advantage of each other. Try to find the best way of making as many of each other's goals come true as possible.

Once you start, there will be many opportunities to help each other. While such a confrontation may bring out disagreements, it will also reveal areas of great mutuality that previously may not have been emphasized as much as on your first list.

Even in a marriage one must sometimes use some of the tactics described earlier. Nobody is perfect, and no one is married to someone who is reasonable, mature, and giving all of the time. When you find yourself dealing with a childish, petulant, arrogant, or nasty spouse who is glowering in the shadows, waiting to pounce on you, you do yourself a disservice by not establishing your territorial limits. If you don't, you may try to assert control in worse ways, perhaps by pretending you feel ill or by not responding to the other's needs.

Be Direct

There is no better way of handling an unreasonable husband or wife than by being direct and straightforward. You don't get as angry, you don't hold the anger in. The anger doesn't build up, and you can be usually decent and friendly again in a while.

Look at this typical party scene: Ben's been drinking too much and telling off-color stories loudly. His wife, Sandra, is getting upset, as she always does when he acts this way. She says nothing and waits till later that evening to pull her own little dirty joke on Ben, the old headache-at-bedtime routine. He's unaware of what's going on and just gets angry.

Sometimes she loses her temper at the party:

SANDRA (*in front of everyone*): Okay, Ben, enough! You've made enough of a fool out of yourself.

Exactly wrong! Ben is now trapped in an open conflict. The issue is: who's the boss? All their friends are making mental bets to see who wins. Now Ben feels entitled to become really obnoxious. Sandra then feels entitled to blow her top, and the situation will mushroom way out of proportion to its importance.

The best way to handle this would be for Sandra to take Ben aside and level with him quietly and privately. To attack him in public is unpardonable and almost never justified. When she does level with him, Sandra must be explicit about her real feelings. Her objective is to make him stop, not to punish him! The best way for her to win is to let Ben know that he is hurting her.

SANDRA (*aside*): Look. I want you to know something. You make me very uncomfortable and very angry acting like that and telling this story. If you want to turn me off, keep it up.

BEN: What's the matter? Don't you have a sense of humor?

SANDRA: I hope you have one when we get home (*so he'll know what punishment she is planning*).

No marriage can work without sharp limits being drawn occasionally. It's just wishful thinking to expect that everything can always go well without taking a stand to make sure that it does. Just in case you need some examples of how to be firm, here are a few of people putting the old foot down to establish limits.

SHE: I've had it! You can't go running out whenever you want. Look at all the organizations you belong to. Let's stop fooling each other. You belong to them just so you can get out of the house. If you want to get out you can, but all the time is ridiculous.

or:

HE: We're not going out with the Blakes anymore. I cannot stand that woman! I know she is your friend and you are entitled to keep her. But I will not ruin the only night in the week we go out by spending it in her company.

or:

SHE: I'm sorry you feel that my place is in the home all the time. I don't feel that way. I have friends to visit. I have a job offer that interests me, and for once you're going to have to make an adjustment to the way I want to live. I'm a person too!

The examples are endless. Find what you want to do, what you must have to make you happy, and put your foot down, dammit! Remember: if you don't feel like a winner in your own marriage, it's unlikely that you are really able to give your spouse what he/she needs: the care, the love, the attention, and the interest that make living with another person worthwhile. If you feel you are a loser in your marriage, you can be certain that your spouse does, too.

When a partner feels like a loser in a marriage, he is eventually going to do something that makes him/her feel like a winner outside of the marriage. If you're smart, you'll look at your present circumstances, see what you can give, demand, and receive. If you can get more of what you want, you'll be able to give more, and vice versa. But you must try, and straightforwardly. And now!

21 / EVERYTHING YOU ALWAYS WANTED TO KNOW ABOUT WINNING AT SEX

MORE HAS BEEN written about sex in the past few years than is probably helpful or necessary. There are manuals, journals, magazines, movies, and therapies. The list is huge and growing rapidly. Everyone is looking for answers.

What does it all boil down to? Simply this: In spite of all the positions, devices, techniques, and clinics, the most important ingredient in a happy sex life is loving the other person and being loved by him in a way that allows for growth, individual freedom, and taste. Without this, you don't have anything. With love you can generally learn to be open with the other person and you can help each other find the way.

The sex faddists have drastically missed the boat. People aren't looking for sex; they're looking for someone to end their feeling of loneliness. If you are interested in sex, you can find it everywhere; any corner of any small town will yield its supply of sexual activity in all forms. It's there if you want it. But acceptance and an end to loneliness are not.

To be sexually satisfied means that you and the person you love have accepted each other. The erotic urgency that the manuals try to sell has little to do with acceptance or satisfaction. Such feelings are characteristically found at the beginning of a relationship and are related to the feeling of novelty. You cannot reasonably expect any long-term relationship to maintain the feeling of newness that it radiated at the beginning. It is possible to keep a love alive, but rarely with that old special fire, because that old special fire is the feeling of discovering of someone new.

It's foolish for a couple to blame each other because that old excitement has gone. Time is the real villain. Let's face it: learning a new sexual technique is not going to make two people stop hating each other and start feeling what they once felt for each other. A playwright said "You'll do anything for someone you once loved, except to love them again." The form of love changes with the years, and so do people; you can learn a new way to love the way a person grows and changes, but that's still not the same feeling.

Much of the new sexual interest sounds like an appeal to everyone's hidden wish to recapture his youth, to be free of responsibility, to have a second chance. That is a lovely thought, but it can be very destructive to a marriage. It makes it increasingly difficult to enjoy the acceptance that you do have and to learn how to be more accepting and understanding of the person you love, because you end up comparing the other person to an impossibly perfect, ever-new standard that is always beyond reach.

Don't get me wrong. There's nothing wrong with learning something new about sex, provided you aren't using that as a substitute for the simple things: being kind to each other, giving each other the benefit of the doubt, and realizing the other's human limitations. You should take into account the fact that your fantasies aren't always fulfillable, even when the other person is willing. People often protect themselves by making impossible demands that they could not meet themselves, knowing that they will be refused by their partner before they have a chance to fail in their own eyes.

Sex is nothing more than a game. You can play by whatever rules you want. In the long run, what gives the most pleasure is sharing a feeling of closeness with a special person, just being together, and not being lonely.

The rest . . . the rest is just anybody's game.

A CHILD NEEDS a home where he knows he will always be let in and accepted simply because he is himself. He needs to know that he is loved, whether he is still wetting the bed, soiling his pants, messing up the table, breaking ashtrays, tearing linen, or hitting other children, and that his parents believe he'll turn out fine. He must understand that he makes others irritated at him when he does "bad" things, but *that does not mean that he is "bad."* It means that what he does is annoying or painful to others.

If children feel loved for being themselves, they can gather their forces to overcome adversity. And later, when they achieve success, they are not left feeling empty and alone.

When a child learns that he can expect to be loved, he has learned what it means to be human, and then both he and his parents have won.

A child should never be made to feel that it is his duty to raise the fallen standard of parental hopes that never materialized. He should not be made to feel that it's his responsibility to excel where his parents could not, nor be used to prove by doing so that, had they had his opportunities, his parents also could have succeeded. A child should not be forced to fulfill his parents' dreams in an attempt to prove that their self-image was not a figment of their imagination; he will become lost in doing so and may find himself becoming a stranger to his own sense of reality.

THERE IS NO special secret for managing professional people. They are people like everyone else and they are perfectly capable of committing the same blunders. That's very important to remember, because *they* sometimes forget it.

It's not difficult to see how professionals manage to become so wrapped up in themselves. Their training takes years of effort, study, and dedication, and they tend to believe that the way they see the world is the only possible way. What is even more troublesome is that they are often so involved in the logic and language of their profession that they take for granted that everyone else understands them.

Since you hire professionals to solve problems that you can't manage, you may not understand much of what they tell you. It is *your* responsibility to ask questions. One of the things that makes the management of professionals so awkward is the all-too obvious fact that you consulted them to manage something that you could not. In some way you feel at their mercy when everything is confused, and hope they will get you out of an unpleasant situation or solve a problem without your help. Yes, your help! When you feel they are doing something wrong, you generally feel inhibited about confronting them; you like to think that they know what they're doing and you're afraid to find out otherwise. But remember: you're not *supposed* to know anything about their profession. So what can you lose in their eyes if you ask?

With professionals you can only lose by not asking.

The following is a situation with a doctor, but any professional could be substituted.

DOCTOR'S OFFICE

DOCTOR: Well, that about completes the preliminary tests.

PATIENT: What's wrong? Do you know yet?

DOCTOR (*not sure*): Well, it's hard to tell. A lot of your tests were, well, just borderline—neither here nor there. It's awfully hard to say one way or the other.

PATIENT: I see. (*She doesn't.*)

DOCTOR: Let's see if there was anything special. (*Looks through her chart again*) Hmmm. That one I don't like.

PATIENT (*holding her breath*): What's that?

DOCTOR: Well, this X-ray report. (*reads*) Some indication of scarring in the cardia. Hmm (*mumbles*). Could be an old problem there. Might be acting up now. (*He's still not sure.*)

The doctor is looking at a report of a series of X-rays which he took of this woman's upper gastro-intestinal system to see whether she had ulcers. The cardia is part of the stomach. She doesn't know that. She thinks the doctor is talking about her heart.

PATIENT (*frightened*): My God! I don't understand this.

DOCTOR (*surprised at her reaction, thinking she is an overreactor*): Now, now, Mary (*in a calming doctor voice*). We can't let ourselves get upset over something like that. It's nothing that can't be managed.

PATIENT (*not liking the way she's being handled for what she thinks is such a serious problem, her heart condition*): But I thought you said the problem was just my nerves (*frantic*)!

DOCTOR: It probably still is. I think your stomach complaints come from swallowing too much air. People do that when they get nervous (*writing out a prescription*). These will help.

PATIENT (*shouting*): But I'm not nervous!

DOCTOR: Look at you, Mary, shouting like that. Come, now. Isn't that being a bit irritable? Sometimes we aren't always aware of what is bothering us, and when the problem has a psychological origin, well, it's even more common.

PATIENT (*confused*): But it's my heart! I don't understand you.

DOCTOR: Don't worry about your heart. It looks just fine on the electrocardiogram. See, Mary, you're concerned about everything but the real problem.

PATIENT (*more confused*): What's that?

DOCTOR: The way you live. Running yourself ragged all over town to do errands. You've got to slow things down. Take it more leisurely. This running isn't doing you any good now, is it?

PATIENT: No, I guess it isn't (*thinking he wants her to rest to take care of her heart*).

DOCTOR: When was the last time you and your husband went away together?

PATIENT (*thinking the question ridiculous*): Last year. We went to the beach for a week.

DOCTOR: Well, you've got to get away more often. (*If she had said she was away last week, he would have told her it wasn't long enough, or that she really didn't relax.*) How are you and Bill getting along these days?

PATIENT: Fine.

DOCTOR: Fine? What do you mean?

PATIENT: Fine! We're getting along fine.

DOCTOR: No problems?

PATIENT: Just the usual. He works hard. I try to keep him pleased.

DOCTOR: Your kids are bigger now?

PATIENT (*sadly*): My baby is in school now.

DOCTOR: You sounded a bit sad saying that.

PATIENT: Well, you know how it is when there aren't any more kids at home. I miss them, I guess. I like the freedom, though.

DOCTOR: Sounds like you're using your freedom to run yourself ragged. You know what, Mary? I think you ought to have another baby.

PATIENT (*really confused*): I don't want another baby!

DOCTOR: It would do you a world of good!

Conversations like this take place every day. A baby is not going to make this patient feel better, nor is a sermon on how to relax. Doctors love to tell patients to relax. *How many doctors do you know who know how to relax?* This woman is upset because she feels she has no purpose in life and is in a turmoil over what to do about it. Her blues aren't associated with menopause, diet, hormonal imbalance, or disease. They are associated with being bored and never having learned to do anything with herself. She's lonely, wants attention, feels useless and believes that her husband doesn't think she is attractive any more. What she needs like a hole in the head is to have another baby. If the doctor thinks she should have another baby, let *him* get pregnant and get up nights to feed it. He has asked the wrong questions and she remained silent.

This woman could have asked the doctor what the word "cardia" meant. She would have been relieved to find that it has nothing to do with the heart. Then she would have been much calmer in the office. She also should have asked the doctor why he felt she should have a baby and why he felt her "nerves" were somehow not as they should be. But she didn't. She expected to be told everything.

Coming Up: The Doctor's Runaround

What you get when you do not ask your physician questions is called the runaround. It's not that they want to avoid the issue, but that many of the problems that they see are not of clearcut physical origin. Many have psychological components. This can be very frustrating. Most physicians try to put your disease into a category and treat it. Medical problems are usually easier to treat than psychological problems, so if you don't object, you'll probably be given medicine (like Mary).

On the other hand, when it is very difficult to establish a medical diagnosis, doctors have a tendency to ascribe symptoms to psychological mechanisms which may or may not be responsible. They say, "It's psychosomatic," and that takes the pressure off them. There have been more psychological mechanisms invented to explain inscrutable medical findings than you could possibly imagine. They make the doctor feel better.

If you are getting a runaround and your doctor continues to tell you that you are having psychological problems, do yourself a favor and see a psychiatrist to find out for sure. Chances are he'll be able to evaluate your case and set your mind at ease. No matter what, don't give up—don't be a stoic! Tell your doctor if you're not getting better.

The cardinal rule for dealing with all professionals is: *never be afraid to ask for another opinion.* Many people do not want to offend their doctor or lawyer or dentist. Yet most professionals welcome the opportunity to have another opinion on the case, especially from a high-powered expert. That way they learn a great deal. They have a chance to see you in a new perspective. And they can share the responsibility. They are usually very happy to give you a list of other professionals and will even make the appointment for you. It's no big deal. If your professional does not want you to have another opinion, you have a very big problem on your hands: your professional is not very sure of himself. Now, knowing that, why should *you* be so sure of *him*?

If you can't get a referral, call the local medical, dental, legal, or other professional association for one. They'll be pleased to help you out.

Seven Rules for Winning with Professionals

1. Be honest with him and tell him as much about your problem as possible. Don't try to cover up your shortcomings and failures. If you were so terrific to begin with, you might not have needed him.

2. He's there to help you, and you're paying for it. Never forget that. You are the judge of whether or not he is helpful. He gives you advice, but it's your decision whether to take it or not.

3. Don't let professionals run your life, and don't trust them with deiisions. You make the decision whether you are going to be operated on. It's your life. It is much easier for a lawyer to convince a client to take the action he wants than it is for him to present all the facts to him and wait for him to make up his own mind. Most lawyers try to be honest and leave the decision to the client.

4. Professionals earn a living by selling their services. If you are considering a lawsuit, your attorney might say you have a 75 percent chance of winning. Do you know what the lawyer for the other side is saying to the other guy? Right! That *he* has a 75 percent chance of winning the case. Who's right? Well, you'll find out in court. And that takes legal services. Professionals frown on anyone doing what they do without benefit of degree, even if they do it well. Accountants think all people need accountants. The professional outlook is to find a need for services, to sell them, and to do it right, by the book—their book. All professionals have rules, and many of the rules seem to be more for the protection of the profession than for the people they serve.

5. Remember, a professional is your employee. He works for you. You hire his services. If you don't like what he is doing, you can fire him.

6. Whenever possible, ask your professional for his opinion, why he believes it, and what he feels should be done about it. Are there alternatives? What will it cost? How long will it take? How successful does he think his plan will be over any other, and why?

7. Professionals need to be managed like everyone else. Because they tend to get very defensive when their expertise is questioned, you must be diplomatic in bringing in ideas that might put them off. It is very irritating for a patient to walk into a doctor's office waving a copy of an article from a medical journal saying, "I want you to give me these pills." The proper approach is to say, "I have seen an article about a pill that is being used. Could you tell me what you think of it and whether you think it might be helpful to me?"

Always remember: professionals are professionals and need to be approached in this way. Just because you are a layman doesn't mean you don't have common sense; just do start using it. The best professionals are sure of themselves and are not threatened if you suggest a new medication or draft a contract or work out a bookkeeping system or make a suggestion for a change in the blueprints. Those who are less sure of themselves dread being shown up by others, often because their skill and expertise is less than it might be, so that the difference between them and the layman is less.

You have a right to know all of these answers. If you don't, you just may find them out the hard way. . . .

With a professional, you must try to find out what you are getting into *every step of the way*. Don't sit there like a dummy. Ask questions.

HERE'S A FAMILIAR PROBLEM: the grandparents are dropping in without calling first.

Episode 1

HUSBAND: It's the door, dear! I'll get it.

WIFE: God, I bet it's your parents again. It's time for the kids' supper. That's when they always come by.

HUSBAND: Oh, Hi, dad. Hi, mom!

DAD: (*walking by husband as if he were invisible*) Where are the kids?

MOM: Here, dear! (*gives a kiss on the cheek, without looking at husband*)

Hi, Helen. (*calling to granddaughter*)

HELEN: Grandma! Grandma! It's Grandma, Billy!

BILLY (*getting up from the dinner table and running out*): Yeah!

WIFE (*under her breath*): Traitors!

HUSBAND: How've you been?

MOM (*ignoring comment*): Hello, Billy! Billy boy, Look what Grandma's got for you!

DAD: And look what we've got for Helen.

HUSBAND: Would you like me to take your coats?

DAD: No, no, we'll only stay a minute.

MOM (*taking off her coat*): Are you people eating?

For the last eight years, at least twice a week, the grandparents have been dropping by at suppertime, unannounced. Invariably, they act surprised that the family is eating. Invariably, they have no intention of staying or eating. Invariably, they stay and eat:

WIFE (*getting her kiss on the cheek from her mother-in-law. It should be pointed out that wife and husband have been married for only eight years, so she has not been completely accepted by her in-laws yet.*) Yes, we're eating.

MOM (*lifting a pot lid*): That looks nice, what is it?

WIFE: Campbell's chicken noodle soup.

MOM: From a can? I could have brought over some soup I made myself. Here's some meatballs I made.

WIFE (*taking the bowl, putting it in the refrigerator*): Thank you.

DAD: Aren't you going to try them? (*takes the bowl out of the refrigerator*) Here try this (*hands a fork with a piece of meatball to wife*).

WIFE (*trapped*): Well. Okay. That's very good. But I've already made dinner.

MOM: That's okay (*starts taking out plates*).

Mother has managed, in her own subtle way, to make the wife feel guilty because the wife is angry and can't express it. If the wife refuses to go along she will seem inhospitable. The way the situation is allowed to develop, she cannot win. No one has established the ground rules. If she goes along with the parents, she ends up making a bigger meal, upsetting the children's bedtime routine, increasing the work she has to do, making her day three hours longer.

This aggravation, combined with the strain of getting angry and upset and feeling guilty, often leads to having words with her husband, who is in no better shape.

HUSBAND (*to his father*): How's everything going?

A dangerous question when you want to keep a visit as short as possible. Parents have a tendency to complain about everything when they have a chance, especially their health. Complaining is no good for them or for their children. It only leads to pointless, helpless discussions about how they are getting older and can't do as much as they used to. Which is depressing to them and to their children, as well as upsetting to their grandchildren.

Soon they complain about not having enough money, no matter how well off they are, and about their health; that is, death and dying. Such parents often attempt to maintain the same control over their children as they did years ago. To be able to control the children symbolically means that they are not old and that they are not losing control over life:

FATHER: I don't know how much longer I can keep working like this (*presses hand across his chest*). Don't tell your mother, but I really get tired a lot of the time.

HUSBAND: Oh, have you seen someone?

FATHER (*insulted*): Why should I see someone? You mean a doctor? There's nothing wrong with me!

To attempt to respond to these self-contradictory statements in a situation like this only provokes conflict. These parents will play both sides of the fence, trying to maintain control. They wrap their children up in guilt. They have the husband up a tree. He's sitting in the living room trying to be hospitable while also trying to think of ways to calm his wife down. She frantically tries to make the salad bigger, put another leaf in the table, then reset it for two more places, and invent some side dishes. She's so angry that she wouldn't use the in-laws' meatballs if hell froze over. The dog will have a treat tonight!

A lovely evening is in store for the two of them. The parents are sitting in the living room giving the husband the reports of their last medical examinations (for the third time this month) and complaining about their expenses again. Father still won't take his coat off. The husband feels like an idiot.

How do you win in a situation like this? The answer is, you don't. You can only lose. What is worse, the more you try to win, to resist them after they've arrived, the more you lose. You'll feel more guilty the more you complain. Just imagine how you'd feel if you refused to let them in and watched them walk away downcast, especially if one of your kids started calling after them to stay.

Here's How To Control the In-Laws

If parents drop in infrequently that's one thing, but when they make a daily practice out of it, it is another. You have rights. You'd like to stop it. There is a way.

Whose responsibility is it to set affairs straight? Each partner should deal with his own parents unless it is too difficult for him to do. To do otherwise could alienate both partners. It will be difficult at best. Accept it. It is going to be unpleasant and you may even feel guilty, but you will feel less so if you follow the simple rules. Recite your rights. State the obvious. Put the burden on their shoulders, where it belongs. After all, you aren't the ones who are at fault.

TELEPHONE CALL

HUSBAND: Dad . . .

FATHER: Hi, how are all of you?

HUSBAND: Fine, just fine.

FATHER: How are all the kids?

HUSBAND: Fine, Dad. I . . .

FATHER: How's little Helen? And that wiseguy Billy boy?

HUSBAND: Fine. They're both fine.

FATHER: You sure nothing's wrong? (*Aside to Mother*) He says everything's okay. Be quiet and let me talk to him.

HUSBAND: Look, I have to talk to you.

FATHER: Something *is* the matter? Is it the kids? Is that why you called?

HUSBAND: No. Please listen for a minute.

FATHER: I won't say a word.

MOTHER (*in background*): What's wrong?

FATHER: I don't know.

MOTHER: Let me talk with him!

FATHER: No! Wait a minute!

HUSBAND (*beside himself*): Look, will you let me talk? First, this conversation is going to be unpleasant, so try and understand. Sally and I really enjoy your company. We really do, and the children love to see you. But when you come over without calling you make a lot of extra work and upset the children's schedule. And you always come over at meal time. So you should call first.

Okay, now watch the response he's going to get. The whole guilt thing. They will immediately withdraw from the battle. The father will say he knows when he's not wanted and will offer not to come over again, ever. Besides, what difference does it make, since, he'll say, he's going to die soon? This sort of comment is designed to give a sense of over-kill so that you will react against it and end up precisely where you were before.

FATHER: Well! Then I think that your mother and I shouldn't come over at all anymore, if that's the way you feel. It'll be easier for me. The traveling is too much at my age anyway.

I told you so! Well, what do you do? Do you retreat to the position that you've had all along, to the situation that you can't stand? To do so would make it even more difficult to bring the point up again. So:

> HUSBAND: We do like to see you, but we'd like you to call. It gets all confusing.
> MOTHER (*in background*): It's *her* idea! I know it! I know when I'm not wanted.

Look, you're fighting this the wrong way. Their weapon is controlling you with guilt. Your weapon can be *your* use of guilt. You must be scratching your head. Guilt from where? How? Watch this approach:

> HUSBAND: Well, I didn't want to tell you this because I didn't want to get you worried, or to feel guilty about coming over.
> FATHER: What are you talking about? What's wrong?
> HUSBAND: On the days you come over, Helen and Billy get so excited that they eat too quickly and run around wildly, because they love you so much and they're impossible to manage the next day. Billy does very poorly in school when he's tired and can't concentrate. The teacher has been sending us notes about it.

The shoe is suddenly on the other foot. Often the same parents who do not believe that their own children have rights feel very strongly that their grandchildren do. They may feel put upon when they are asked to comply with their children's wishes, but they feel obligated to do what's best for the grandchildren.

Must You Always Give In?

To those of you who dislike subterfuge, who protest that you should be able to say what you want to to your parents, I say,

"Why haven't you, up until now?" If you haven't, it's probably because you are caught in a similar kind of guilt. You want to act but are afraid of hurting, of being rejected, of being hurt. These are parents with whom one can be more direct. But it is human nature that, as people grow older, they become preoccupied with death, less interested in the rights of anyone but themselves. All they want, they say, is a little enjoyment before they die.

Even if this were true, it is no reason to give into their demand that events always go their way. By always giving in, you are in a sense agreeing with them that their time is limited —and this is frightening to them. Look at it this way: *you* could get killed tomorrow!

When parents withdraw they sometimes make their children responsible for keeping them in touch with the world. The worst thing you can do for such parents is to take away their sense of autonomy, their sense of control over their world. But to allow them to take over your life in order to keep them from withdrawing is unrealistic. It does not help them. It only gives them a false sense of control in a situation that is at best ambivalent.

It is possible to state the facts to parents very simply. That is not the problem. The problem is to anticipate their withdrawal and to deal with it. The following introductory remarks may be useful:

"I have something to discuss with you. I'd like you to try to understand how I feel about this problem and realize that it has nothing to do with you personally. I don't want you to get hurt and back away by taking this the wrong way. And I wouldn't mention it unless it were important to me."

They'll probably still withdraw. Don't argue. Be pleasant, but be firm.

Even if your parents are usually open, warm and giving, they will still be unpleasant to deal with when you try to limit them. This is just a function of growing older. Generally, when parents still maintain a life and world of their own that fulfills them, they are much easier to manage. The answer to your parents' intruding on your life may not be in dealing with the intrusion itself, but in helping them find new outlets outside their family to satisfy and fulfill themselves.

Even though you think pointing out to your parents what bothers you should be sufficient to get them to change, it usually is not. Parents believe that they have earned the right to have their way. They often feel that their time has come and that they should be repaid for their earlier disappointments in life before it's too late.

What Family Functions Are Unavoidable?

Another common difficulty that grown children encounter with their parents is being expected to go to endless family functions. Parents are frequently very rigid in their ideas about this and are unwilling to bend. If there are very few functions in your family and your attendance is important enough so that you truly would be missed (and more than just in the sense that you were not there), you might as well take a deep breath and resign yourself to going. Think of it this way: since you're needed, you'd feel so guilty by not going that it would interfere with your function elsewhere. Remember: guilt has a way of making one ruin one's efforts and opportunities. By winning (in your eyes), by refusing to go, you may actually be setting yourself up for an interminable battle with your relatives or for feeling so guilty that you'll be the loser in the end.

It's a rare person who can't tolerate attending *one* Christmas dinner; *one* Easter dinner, *one* Thanksgiving dinner. But some families have rituals of congregating that are seemingly endless. If your family is like that and you wish to get out of going to four or five Christmas dinners or a dozen visits at Thanksgiving, then the problem is considerable.

The motive behind the need to assemble is often the

parents' wish to feel complete, respected, or worthwhile. Gathering the clan together is how they reassure themselves. It is a display rather than a dinner, a show of strength rather than a social event. So it is a matter that must be handled carefully if you wish to make any changes in your participation.

WIFE: Mom, I want to talk to you about the big dinner.

MOTHER: The one at our house or Clara's or the Lamberts'?

WIFE: Well, all of them. I've been talking it over with Tom and we both feel it's just too much to do.

MOTHER: What are you talking about?

Mother believes that it is her right that her daughter attend; and look how fast she defends that right. First parental ploy: To compare the "delinquent" child with other siblings. They act hurt:

MOTHER: Your sister is planning to go and to bring her children to our house.

WIFE: Oh, I plan to go to your house for Christmas dinner, but Clara's and the Lamberts', well I'm drawing the line there. We won't be going.

MOTHER: I don't understand!

This is the second ploy: It's never been done before, so how come you're doing it now? And if you do it now, you could do it again.

MOTHER: You used to *love* Aunt Clara's when you were a little girl. Remember?

Parents tend to fall back on you *"you used to"* thinking when they deal with their children; this is the way they brought them up. It's like teaching a kid to eat squash. You get him to try it once and if he eats it you say, "See, you ate it, you must like it. It wasn't that bad, was it? Have some more." This coercive adaptation to parental standards is extended to other issues. The fact that a child has once done something, even if under pressure, is accepted as proof that the child wished to do it, whether or not in fact he did. Everything is fine when these children do as expected, but if they want to change, all hell breaks loose. It is as if tradition implies consent and consent implies appetite. But to pursue The Great Christmas Dinner Debate . . .

MOTHER: I can't understand you. You adore Aunt Clara. And the Lamberts have always been wonderful to you.

A new guilt ploy: Parents feel you are supposed to owe something to other people for being good to you even—if you never wanted anything from them, even if they didn't care whether you wanted what they gave you or not. Giving freely shouldn't obligate anyone. To continue:

WIFE: It's just too much. I get very worn out by all these dinners, and the kids scream. It's all unnecessary.

Hold it! Get ready: One of the big guilt ploys is about to be played . . .

MOTHER: Well, what am I supposed to say? How am I going to handle this? What do you think Clara will say when you're not there? What do you think she'll feel about *me*?

Now it's mother's image that will be ruined. *You're* doing it to her! Do you believe this? I hope not. Mother is doing it to herself. Here's how to handle her:

WIFE: I'll call Clara myself. It's not your problem. I'll tell Clara that you had nothing to do with it.

MOTHER: You'll do no such thing! You want everyone to think I brought you up not to respect your mother's wishes?

Another favorite:

MOTHER: Please do it for me. Is that asking too much?

WIFE: I'm already going to one dinner for you. What about me?

Another big ploy:

MOTHER: I can't tell you how upsetting this is to me and how upsetting this is going to be to your father. You'll have to be the one to tell him. I'm not going to *add to all his problems*. He won't hear this from my mouth.

Makes you feel like you've leaked atomic secrets to the enemy and then joined a traveling porno show, doesn't it? But you're a big girl, you know what you want. You wouldn't dream of adding to mother's weaponry would you? Ha! Of course you would:

WIFE: What kind of problems? Is Dad all right?

You, my dear child, are an idiot for asking. You're playing right into her hands.

MOTHER: He won't be after he hears this. You know . . . oh, forget it. It's not important. He doesn't want you to worry about him.

Hold on to your hats . . . big, big ploy:

WIFE: What? Tell me!!

MOTHER: You know how concerned your father is about his health, how worried he is. Well, he's been ruminating over the idea that this may be the last Christmas for him and . . .

She's got you! Zap! Except you forget: he's been pulling that routine for ten years now; he thinks every Christmas is the last one. The fact is that as most people get older they are concerned with dying and worry about how much time they've got left, but that's no excuse to use it as a weapon. Look: you are going to die, too, but you don't use it as an excuse for getting people to act the way you want them to; actually they'd laugh at you. Children don't laugh at their parents when they use this excuse because they've worried about it since they were kids and still fear it like a child.

How do you deal with a difficult situation like this? It is always difficult getting involved in a long discussion with parents over issues that they don't feel are negotiable, such as their rights *vs.* your rights. There are several ways of handling this. First, you can accept your burden as part of the duty of being a child, even at forty-five, and then set your sights on your kids and vow that they will pay you back for it some day. Or you can avoid being around at the time of the dinners by taking a vacation or by arranging a "previous" engagement. If you want this to work, you've got to make arrangements a *long* time in advance. And neither of these plans is really being honest.

The way to deal with parents who are fixed in their ways is not to try to change their way of thinking. It's not possible, so don't attempt it. All you will get is a recitation of the old arguments they once used, like: This is the way your sister does it; this is what people expect; and, you love squash because you always eat it. You can't win this one by arguing. Only by *not* arguing can you take the situation by the horns.

TELEPHONE

WIFE: Mother, Tom and I will not be going to Clara's or the Lamberts' this year. We'll be going to your house for Christmas, but that's all.

MOTHER: I don't understand! You always . . .

WIFE: We're not going. I'm sorry, but I'm not free to give you the reasons now. I can't discuss it any further.

MOTHER: Is something wrong?

WIFE: I just cannot discuss this. Please try and understand.

MOTHER: You have to discuss it! What do you mean you can't discuss it? Everyone will be there. What will they think?

WIFE: I'm sorry, I can't go into it. I have to go now. The baby's crying. I'll be speaking with you.

In dealing with parents in a situation like this, it is important to understand that it is impossible to be truthful with them all of the time, because the truth, no matter how well-founded or how presented, is going to hurt them and make you feel guilty. I suppose you could say it's their problem, which it is, but to argue with them and hurt them and feel guilty about it makes it your problem because you are the one who ends up feeling lousy. You should be very clear about what you can and cannot tell your parents. You might even make a list of subjects to avoid.

You should attempt to set limits and to enforce them by acting clearly and definitively when they are trespassed. While this does not sound too different from setting limits in other situations, it is. It's one thing to keep a neighbor from dropping in at mealtimes. You can lay down the law by telling him he's upsetting your routine and is a pain in the neck. But try saying this to your parents! It doesn't work. What's more, it will cause bad feelings. Put the parents' breach of limits in terms of something about which they are themselves concerned.

If you tell them that their visits may be responsible for their grandchildren's poor school behavior, that might get the job done. What's more, the parents may feel they are actually doing good by complying with your request.

Some people's parents are so headstrong, unreasonable, and unthinking that they are extraordinarily difficult to deal with. These parents do not seem to hear their children's complaints when these are brought up. They are addicted to intruding on the life of their children, to such an extent that it is sometimes difficult for the children to tell whose life they're leading! The best way to manage such parents is to get some physical distance between yourself and them.

Could the Parent Problem Be Your Own Fault?

Before you begin to try to limit your relatives' incursions into your life you must take a long and penetrating look at yourself. Ask whether perhaps you have secretly encouraged some of this parental interference. Is it possible that you may really want this contact in spite of protests to the contrary? Are you really afraid of being on your own? How much do you need your parents? I mean just that, and I'm directing this comment to adults, not teenagers.

Everyone plays some role in inviting troublesome guests, no matter what the situation is. If you were certain that you did not want the guests around, you would have been able to act quickly and turn them away at the door. When the uninvited guest turns out to be a parent, feelings are less clear cut, but it is possible to set some limits and to let them know that you just don't want them around all the time. After all, *they* didn't want *you* around all the time, did they?

Unless you have made a decision to set limits with relatives you aren't going to get anywhere. If you decide you want your mother to stop calling the house all day, or to stop dropping over, inviting herself in and making herself "useful" by doing all of the chores that you should be doing, then you must take a stand.

TELEPHONE CALL—THE SEVENTH THAT DAY

DAUGHTER: Mother, I'm sorry, you must stop calling the house all the time. It's unnecessary.

MOTHER: What does that mean? You don't want to talk to me. Is that what it means?

DAUGHTER: Not this often! God, that's more than I ever talked to you when I was in grade school. I can't be running up and down stairs taking care of the baby and cooking and answering your phone calls.

MOTHER: Maybe you need some help. I can come over and . . .

DAUGHTER: No, I also don't want you coming over any more, not for a while. It takes me long enough to get my work done as it is.

MOTHER: You're telling me I get in the way!

Ha! Big Point!

DAUGHTER: Yes! That's it exactly! You get in my way.

Go ahead: state the obvious! State the obvious and mean it! Hooray!

MOTHER (*sadly*): I guess I'll just hang up.

Another Very Big Point! This is a time to keep your mouth shut. Please! Mother is making a big appeal for sympathy. Okay, there are some additional facts that bother you. Mother is lonely. Older people do get lonely. They start to sit around and read the obituary column first thing in the morning and feel sorry for themselves. By giving them sympathy you play into their self-pity and make it more difficult for them to act otherwise. By acting like the obedient child who tolerates all their phone calls and impromptu visits, you actually encourage them. By not setting limits, you *reward* them for intruding.

The less you complain, the more they'll visit, the more frequently they will call.

It's about this time that mother unleashes her special comments, guaranteed to make her daughter feel guilty. Listen—

MOTHER: Am I asking so much of you? Is it such a big thing for a daughter to speak with her mother every day?

DAUGHTER: What is there in my life that is so fascinating? I'm a drudge like anyone else.

Hold it! Wrong point: Mother is *lonely*, not curious.

MOTHER: What is it? Don't you care about me anymore? You'd think that there'd be a *little* love left. Am I such a bother?

Don't continue. The conversation could go on forever and usually does. There is only one way to stop it, and that is to stop it.

DAUGHTER: I'm not going to call you every day. I'm not on report to you. I am not going to take your calls and stay on the phone with you. I just refuse. You've overdone it.

Rule: Be firm, but NEVER GET ANGRY, no matter how much you are baited.

MOTHER: Well, I just don't know what I'll do. I guess if you don't want to talk to me, I don't want to talk to you.

Rule: Don't take such a parent's threats seriously. If you do, she will feel the need to act on them. Not taking such a threat seriously allows the other person to back down, and not only in this situation.

DAUGHTER: Well, that's silly. I just will not speak to you every day. I don't think there's much else to discuss now. I'll call you on Friday.

MOTHER: I won't be in.

The point is to end the conversation there. Don't linger; keep the discussion short. You should understand beforehand that it won't be easy.

Why Parents Make You Feel So Guilty

In dealing with parents it is important to remember that one always tends to act like a child with them and to become angry and unreasonable. Be firm, be definite, know what you want, and set your limits and act on them. Expect them to make you feel guilty, but no matter how much guilt you feel, do not allow it to run you. This parent-child guilt has a way of getting out of control, causing one side to give up and then try again. If parents see that guilt works once, they will break the limits once more. Each time it gets harder to stop, and each time you lose more and feel guiltier because you feel angrier.

The more you argue with your parents, the more you become like the child they expect you to be. *Parents have a way of making their children act childish.* Be firm; be gentle. Stick up for your rights, but don't be ridiculous about it. Don't be a sucker for any argument based on, "You'll be sorry when we're dead." It never solves anything. Besides, they may outlive you.

It can be equally upsetting to manage brothers and sisters, but here it's feelings of competition that make life miserable. All brothers and sisters compete with each other for their parents' love at one time or other, and most kids feel "Mom liked everyone but me," even though they know better. As a result all kids tend to grow up with some feelings of jealousy about their siblings, a gnawing suspicion that their parents gave the other kids more and that they have been cheated, even if it's never discussed openly. Cinderella is such a popular fairy tale because every child identifies with the mistreated daughter who is being robbed by her sisters of her chance at happiness.

Never do these rivalrous feelings become more apparent than at a time of a family crisis like sickness or death or financial failure. The idea of the family drawing close together at such times is more myth than fact. Brothers and sisters find themselves trying to play the role of the good child and to avoid playing the role of the bad one.

TELEPHONE CALL

LINDA: What's happened to *you?*

PAULA: What do you mean?

LINDA: You haven't been to visit Mother for *the last two days.*

PAULA: I went every day last week (*defending herself, feeling sheepish*).

LINDA: Well so did I, but I also went every day this week!

PAULA: Tommy's been sick and . . .

LINDA: Mother really missed you. We talked about it.

PAULA: That's just great. I only missed one day.

LINDA: You know she's not feeling well, and the last two days have been *especially* rough (*rubbing it in*).

PAULA: What's wrong?

Linda will go on for a half hour telling Paula why she is a bad daughter. Paula should point out Linda's two-faced approach and tell her that she is putting her down.

PAULA: Look, Linda. Cut it out! You're a big girl. I know Mother is not feeling well. Mother doesn't feel well most of the time. If she was having an especially rough day, as you say, why didn't you call me? I would have come right over. And frankly I think sitting with mother and talking about what a miserable person I am for not visiting her only makes her more miserable. You're just upsetting her when you do something like that. Remember what the doctor said: don't upset her. You probably undid all the good your visit accomplished.

Other equally upsetting episodes occur after a parent's death, when the parents' possessions are being divided. The children may be talking about the possessions, but they are also trying to equate which of them was loved the most with the number of possessions they end up with.

When siblings fight, they usually fight like children. The best way of handling brothers and sisters is to accept the competitiveness built into the relationship, to rise above the conflict and play the role of an adult instead of a child. Since it is common to feel cheated and competitive in all interactions with brothers and sisters, be certain that you question your feelings before you decide on any action. Are those feelings the same ones that have been present for years between you and your siblings? Or are they feelings that arise from the situation at hand? To act upon old feelings or feelings that cannot be supported by present situations is to act like a child again and only makes you seem unreasonable and impulsive. A good rule is to focus attention on what is happening now, not on what you felt years ago. Remember, your siblings probably feel the same way you do about the past.

Six Rules for Dealing with Relatives

Here are some points to keep in mind when dealing with relatives.

1. Remember that you have rights, no matter what the circumstances are. Define those rights to yourself. Basically, you have a right to be you, to like what you like and want what you want. You don't owe anyone explanations for why you are you.
2. Relatives have rights. Define them also—where they begin, where they leave off.
3. Know your limits of tolerance with your relatives and be prepared to assert your rights before those limits are reached, when you're still in control of your temper. If you act too soon you'll seem to be acting unfairly. If you wait too late, you'll be too angry to act and may get trapped.
4. Even if you're wrong, you are entitled to have your way at reasonable intervals.
5. Even if they're wrong, they're sometimes entitled to have their way.
6. Don't use reasons 4 and 5 as excuses for not asserting your rights.

Now you know what it takes and you're on your way.

No one promised you it would be easy. If you still think that winning is going to be easy, you haven't learned your lesson yet.

Perhaps you feel that there is something contrived, something artificial about these techniques of winning. Perhaps you think people should just go ahead and do whatever comes naturally. That might have worked once, but urban life *has* become artificial in many respects. It is doubtful that man was ever intended to live so close to other men for so long.

In simpler days when life was less complex, man had to contend with the forces of nature and with the people who threatened him and his property; and while he may have been helpless in the face of nature, he was at least aware of what was going on, and he knew who his enemies were, too.

The forces that threatened our ancestors (and the actions they took to protect themselves) grew more obscure as they became more civilized, more urban. Threats were no longer clear-cut. Enemies could be anywhere and appear just like anyone else. As he became more civilized, man lost the ability to discern what threatened him. In the time it took to tell, he often lost the initiative to correct faults as they developed and to cope with threats before they became overwhelming.

This book is an attempt to help you regain the initiative that society has taken away. It is an attempt to reawaken your perception, to give you new descriptions of your potential enemies, and to show you how to manage them. It tries to help you come to terms with the present condition of man, to make the best of it, to help you find what you want in the world, how to get it, and how to keep it.

Most of all, this book attempts to help you discover that you are your own worst enemy and how to win over yourself.